Dr. **Joseph Levey** is an active jazz performer in the Columbus area (tenor sax and woodwind doubles) who has also performed in back-up bands for such entertainers as John Davidson, Buddy Greco, Nancy Ames, Carmen McRae, and Leslie Uggams. A jazz composer and arranger whose scores have been performed by the highly acclaimed Ohio State Jazz Ensemble, Dr. Levey is former director of the group and is currently director of the Jazz Studies program at Ohio State, where he also is a professor of music.

Prentice-Hall International, Inc., *London*
Prentice-Hall of Australia Pty. Limited, *Sydney*
Prentice-Hall Canada Inc., *Toronto*
Prentice-Hall of India Private Limited, *New Delhi*
Prentice-Hall of Japan, Inc., *Tokyo*
Prentice-Hall of Southeast Asia Pte. Ltd., *Singapore*
Whitehall Books Limited, *Wellington, New Zealand*
Editora Prentice-Hall do Brasil Ltda., *Rio de Janeiro*

Joseph Levey

THE *JAZZ* EXPERIENCE

A GUIDE TO APPRECIATION

A SPECTRUM BOOK

Prentice-Hall, Inc., Englewood Cliffs, New Jersey 07632

Library of Congress Cataloging in Publication Data

Levey, Joseph.
     The jazz experience.

     "A Spectrum Book"
     Bibliography: p.
     Includes discographies and index.
     1. Jazz music—History and criticism.   2. Jazz music—
Analysis, appreciation.   I.   Title.
ML3506.L48   1983   781'.57   82-24126
ISBN 0-13-510248-0
ISBN 0-13-510230-8 (pbk.)

© 1983 by Joseph Levey

This book is available at a special discount when ordered
in bulk quantities. Contact Prentice-Hall, Inc., General
Publishing Division, Special Sales, Englewood Cliffs, N.J. 07632.

1 2 3 4 5 6 7 8 9 10

ISBN 0-13-510248-0

ISBN 0-13-510230-8 (PBK.)

Editorial/production supervision by Rita Young
Cover design by Hal Siegel
Manufacturing buyer: Pat Mahoney

To Liz:
tireless editor, intrepid critic,
astute counselor, understanding wife.

CONTENTS

PREFACE

This book differs from most jazz texts in that it is not organized chronologically within the framework of jazz history. Instead of using the history of jazz as the means to understanding, it looks at jazz as it is today and locates it within the broad stream of American pop music. It identifies the components of most American pop music and shows how jazz has used the popular idiom throughout its existence. It analyzes the organizational elements of jazz, identifies jazz as an international music, introduces key figures and major influences, and assists the reader in becoming a discerning jazz listener.

The book is designed to move from the general to the specific, with the aim of guiding the reader toward an informed appreciation of jazz. At the end of some chapters there are Suggested Records, Suggestions for Listening, and Suggested Further Readings. The purpose is to encourage the listener to make judgments and formulate conclusions based on a substantive understanding of the art as it exists today.

ACKNOWLEDGMENTS

Excerpt from "Number Twenty-six" by Whitney Balliett in *The New Yorker Magazine* is reprinted by permission; © 1980 The New Yorker Magazine, Inc.

Excerpt from "Overtones" by Malcolm E. Bessom is reprinted by permission of *Music Educators Journal;* © 1980 Music Educators National Conference.

Excerpt from "Griffin" by Zan Stewart is reprinted by permission; © 1979 *Musician, Player & Listener.*

FIRST IMPRESSIONS

Jazz is a uniquely American music, and although it rests solidly within the realm of popular music, it has never had the widespread mass appeal that rock, for example, has had for the generations of the 1950s, 1960s, and 1970s. On the other hand, its many fans range in age from older—indeed, elderly—people who were exposed to jazz during the swing era to young people who may have been only vaguely aware of jazz until they reached a college campus. Jazz enthusiasts span the social and geographical spectrum as well, encompassing black Americans who have a special interest in the music, white Americans of many different origins and backgrounds, and European and Oriental aficionados whose affinity for this particularly American style of music is remarkable. Truly, what began as an ethnic and provincial kind of musical expression has become a popular art form of universal appeal.

INITIAL OBSERVATIONS

The first observation that one might make about jazz is that its devotees are attracted not so much by the visual appearance of the players as by the sound of the music itself. Audiences go to *see* a rock concert, but they attend a jazz concert to *hear* the participants play. Famous jazz stars often appear on stage in casual dress with no make-up, props, special lighting, or choreography. Their musical instruments and a well-adjusted public address system are sufficient. Another related observation that may be made is that because jazz is not created for mass appeal it is usually a more complex, intricate, and thought-provoking music than rock, pop, or country music. It demands the listener's attention and concentration—with commensurate rewards. Although some jazz performers are more theatrical than others, the intent of a jazz performance is not to reach an audience with a show but to reach them through original, inspired playing.

Another simple observation one can make after some thoughtful listening is that jazz, unlike rock or pop or country music, places emphasis on instrumental performance, and singing is of secondary importance in the hierarchy of jazz.

FURTHER OBSERVATIONS

What is there in the general sound of jazz that many listeners find attractive? The first and most basic element is the beat—the regular, repeated pulse that is also present in nearly all other types of American pop music. The drummer, with the pulse-keeping and rhythm-reinforcing instruments, is the important contributor to this effect. An important bass voice (usually a string bass or electric bass) is also present much of the time in jazz music, not only to aid in time keeping but also to support the tonality of the music.

Another distinctive element found in most jazz efforts is rhythmic surprise in the form of *syncopation*. The aforementioned rhythmic pulse combined with rhythmic variety and modification contribute to the natural character of jazz. These rhythmic surprises emanate not only from the rhythm section (drums, keyboard, bass, and rhythm guitar) but are also observable in the ensemble playing and in the individual solos.

A further element of the singular sound of jazz is the kind of instruments usually employed to perform it. Jazz is customarily played with certain wind instruments of the brass and woodwind families, and the necessary instruments to chord and keep time, called the rhythm section. Trumpets and trombones are important jazz voices, but French horns and tubas are seldom used. Saxophones and, to a lesser degree, clarinets and flutes, are important, but oboes and bassoons are rarely heard. In the rhythm section, one drummer will play an assortment of drums and cymbals, and this collection is called a *drum set*. A piano or a similar keyboard instrument is quite important to the rhythm section, and a plucked bass string instrument is included most of the time. As for other stringed instruments, it is apparent that the guitar is very popular, but the violin is employed infrequently for jazz performance and the viola and cello are hardly used at all.

THE BIG BAND AND THE COMBO

Most of the time, jazz is performed by a small group called a *combo* or by a larger group called a *stage band* or a *big band*. A common exception is the solo pianist or solo guitarist. The combo may be as small as a duo (two) or trio (three), or there may be as many as seven, eight, or nine musicians. By comparison, the stage band is a larger ensemble comprised of groups or sections of trumpets, trombones, saxophones, and the rhythm section. The stage band usually plays elaborately written scores called *arrangements* or *charts*. These scores are often original compositions designed to display the colors and nuances of the standard big band. The sound and impact of the large jazz ensemble are forceful and incisive, and many new jazz fans are first drawn to jazz by such a group.

Enthusiasts who are first interested in the stage band may later begin to appreciate the combo as the perfect vehicle for displaying solo improvisations; in the combo there is normally far less emphasis on written music and much more emphasis on the unwritten solos (improvisations). When the novice listener arrives at the point where his or her attention is focused on the solos and soloists, a true understanding of jazz has begun. The soloists are the stars of any jazz performance, and they receive most of the attention and applause.

THE IMPROVISER

The neophyte listener soon discovers that the solo improviser takes liberties with the music, transforming the original theme into a modification or series of modifications. As the soloist improvises, the listener hears variations of the theme; these variations seem to be different and yet musically related to the original theme. For the jazz fan, the impromptu quality of this process is perhaps the most exciting and rewarding part of the presentation.

In rock, pop, or country music, although the instrumentalists do play solos occasionally, the solos are usually a minor part of the presentation. The emphasis is on the singer, who is the star. By contrast, the central feature of jazz is the improvised instrumental solo. (The special role of the jazz singer will be discussed in the next chapter.)

SUGGESTED RECORDS:

CLARK TERRY, *Big B-A-D Band Live.* Vanguard VSD-79355
AKIYOSHI/TABACKIN, *Long Yellow Road.* RCA JPL-1-1350
THAD JONES/MEL LEWIS, *Consummation.* Blue Note BST-84346
HEATH BROTHERS, *Passing Through.* Columbia 35573
OSCAR PETERSON, *The Oscar Peterson Big 6 at the Montreux Jazz Festival, 1975.* Pablo 2310-747
GERRY MULLIGAN, *Gerry Mulligan Quartet.* Vogue 07
BUDDY RICH, *Stick It.* RCA LSP-4802
The Art of the Modern Jazz Quartet. Atlantic SD-2-301

SUGGESTIONS FOR LISTENING:

1. Begin to hear the differences between a combo and a big band.
2. Begin to recognize the sounds of individual instruments, both wind instruments and rhythm section instruments.
3. Hear the *theme,* which is usually presented first, and then hear the variations on the theme. These variations are played by the soloists. This is *jazz improvisation.*
4. Attend a jazz performance or concert and observe the serious jazz fans in the audience. You will see that what interests them most are the solos.

SUGGESTED FURTHER READINGS:

Understanding Jazz, Leroy Ostransky; chapters 1, 2, 3, 4.
Jazz Styles, Mark C. Gridley; chapters 1, 2, 3.
The Jazz Idiom, Jerry Coker: chapters 4, 5.

THE ACTIVE PARTICIPANTS

THE VIRTUOSO IMPROVISERS

Who are the stars, the jazz "names" whose playing is evaluated by the journalists and critics? They are certainly not the business agents, the orchestrators, the section players, or even, in some cases, the leaders. The virtuoso improvisers are the stars. These are highly skilled and creative instrumental musicians whose specialty is improvisation at a virtuosic level. Their primary skill is melody making; they are melodists. They create instantaneous melody with their artistry and with their instruments, within the piece of music they happen to be playing at the moment.

In the jazz idiom the majority of inventors and innovators have historically been and continue to be black American musicians. They invent new musical forms, new instrumental combinations, and new improvisational styles. It is difficult to say, however, that jazz is exclusively black music. Because music is an art that touches people in both a personal and a universal way, jazz, like any other music, is accessible to any performer. He or she synthesizes and modifies, and so does the next performer, and the next, and so on, and it becomes for each a personal means of musical expression. It must, however, be stressed that the formative roots of jazz spring from black American musicians, and the innovators still are mainly black Americans, although jazz does attract skilled musicians of all races and nationalities because of its challenges. The individual is required to extend himself or herself constantly so as to derive the maximum satisfaction from his or her own performance.

JAZZ SINGING AND JAZZ DANCE

In the past fifty years jazz instrumentalists have made radical changes in the way jazz is conceived and played. Such artists as Charlie Parker, Dizzy Gillespie, Thelonious Monk, John Coltrane, Eric Dolphy, and Elvin Jones were remarkable innovators who changed jazz, turned it around, and set it off in new directions. But there have been no comparable giant strides, no redefinitions of the jazz idiom, from the vocal sphere of jazz. Compared to the quantum leaps made by some of the aforementioned instrumentalists, jazz singing is much as it always was. This is a disparity that is difficult to ignore.

There is a fundamental difference between instrumental jazz and jazz singing. A song is at least partially a literary form of expression; instrumental music is an abstract form of expression. Jazz singing involves lyrics, words, and ideas, whereas jazz playing is a purely musical statement. In other words, a song lyric is about something rather specific—"Straight, No Chaser" is not. Thus, the jazz singer is limited improvisationally, at least to a degree, because he or she is locked into the lyrics. A certain number of obligatory words, syllables, and notes are required in order to accommodate them. The instrumentalist does not have to contend with any such limitation and is free to play whatever skill and imagination can create. In spite of such limitations, extraordinary singers such as Ella Fitzgerald, Sarah Vaughan, Mel Torme, Cleo Laine, Joe Williams, and Carmen McRae manage to be stunningly creative with a song. Many other so-called jazz singers could more correctly be called song stylists who improvise, if at all, in a predictable and formula-like manner.

What is it that jazz singers do? They present American pop songs in a jazzy (jazz-like) manner, meaning that they sing the songs with a syncopated, swinging style. They rework the straightforward lead-sheet melody and lyrics into a jazz rhythm style. They may also at times insert free melodic additions or alterations that are not in the original lead sheet. A few adventurous singers will sometimes improvise with the words of a song as well as with the melody. This can be a formidable intellectual challenge both for the singer and for the listener.

Another common kind of jazz singing abandons the lyrics completely and is called *scat singing*. In scat song the singer uses nonsense syllables and vocal sounds, often in imitation of instrumental jazz lines. The effect is that of instrumental statements being sung, with the voice imitating the saxophone or trumpet. It is interesting to note that many of the early scat singers were instrumentalists first. One of the earliest scat recordings, "Heebie Jeebies," was made by Louis Armstrong in 1926. These instrumentalists performed scat mostly because of its novelty.

Although it is true that early jazz players often imitated with their horns such vocalisms as growls, moans, and shouts, the reverse has been the case in the past fifty years or so, with jazz singers being influenced by the instrumental idiom. This is particularly true of the scat style, in which the singer may imitate horn runs, riffs, and quotations.

For all of these reasons—the radical changes brought about by certain progressive instrumentalists, the restraints engendered by the words, and the symbiotic relationship between scat singing and the instrumental idiom—it is difficult and unfair to evaluate jazz singing with the same criteria one would apply to instrumental performance.

Jazz dance is an exciting and genuinely American form of rhythmic body movement which developed as a natural correlative to the music. Musical entertainment on the stage and in films capitalized on jazz dance and elevated it to a popular art form. In films one can trace the growth and subtlety of jazz dance from Bill "Bojangles" Robinson to Fred Astaire to Gene Kelly to Ben Vereen.

Jazz dance has its own aesthetic principles, of course, which have little to do with jazz music. They are separate yet allied arts. The jazz dancer dances *to* jazz music. He or she is involved in keeping time, imitating the jazz drummer, performing licks and variations in a percussion context. Unlike the drummer, however, the dancer must be *seen* to be really appreciated.

Both the jazz singer and the jazz dancer are dependent to some extent on instrumental music for support and inspiration. This does not diminish their accomplishments, but it does indicate that neither is an essential, indispensable ingredient of jazz. Although jazz singers and dancers have historically coexisted with jazz music and although both are creative and expressive arts, they are incidental to the main thrust of this book, which is instrumental jazz performance.

Why aren't there more women in jazz? There are more now than ever before, but the change in attitudes toward female jazz artists has come slowly. From the end of the nineteenth century and until the 1940s, it was not considered genteel for a young lady to play a brass or percussion instrument. Flute, yes; clarinet or saxophone, maybe; piano and violin were acceptable. Therefore, early examples of women in jazz were mostly singers or pianists.

Consider the environment: jazz is performed in public ballrooms, bars, hotels, roadhouses, and nightclubs. And the often unsavory inhabitants of such places should also be considered. None of this would seem to augur an ideal future for a woman. Still, a few did persevere—Marian McPartland and Mary Lou Williams are notable examples.

Finally, it must also be admitted that until recently there was overt male chauvinism in the music business. Fortunately, this problem seems to be disappearing, especially as more female jazz artists are heard in recordings and performances. As a result of the aforementioned impediments, most of the women who were associated with jazz in its formative years were the early blues singers, such as "Ma" Rainey, Bessie Smith, Ida Cox, Mamie Smith, and Ethel Waters, who worked and recorded with jazz bands.

During the heyday of the swing band era, every swing band and dance band had a "girl singer." Some bands used duos (like the Clooney Sisters) or trios (like the Andrews Sisters). They mostly sang the standard/pop tunes of the day. Some of these vocalists became independent singing stars; a few became movie stars. Three well-known examples are Doris Day, Ethel Waters, and Lena Horne. Billie Holiday became a highly publicized example of what the jazz life might do to an unprotected woman. A well-known personality, she received much adverse publicity after being jailed and institutionalized for drug possession.

Here is a small, subjective selection of significant female jazz *instrumentalists:*

Lil Hardin Armstrong was a pianist with King Oliver and Louis Armstrong. She later led bands of her own.
Mary Lou Williams was one of the first well-known women in jazz. She was a creatively modern jazz pianist and arranger/composer.
Ina Ray Hutton led an all-girl swing band in the mid-1930s and later led an all-male band in the 1940s.

Marian McPartland is an English pianist who came to the United States in the 1940s and has become a well-known jazz woman. She continues to teach, play, record, and advocate jazz performance for women.

Margie Hyams played vibes with Woody Herman and George Shearing.

Toshiko Akiyoshi is a jazz pianist and exemplary composer/arranger who, together with her husband, reed-player Lew Tabackin, led one of the most unique big bands of the 1970s.

Joanne Brackeen is a hard-swinging, creative pianist who has worked with Art Blakey, Dexter Gordon, Mike Brecker, Joe Henderson, Stan Getz, and Jack DeJohnette.

Janice Robinson is a thoughtful young trombonist who has played with the Thad Jones–Mel Lewis Band and the original Broadway production of *Ain't Misbehavin'*.

For the past several years a Women's Jazz Festival has been held in Kansas City featuring women jazz artists who perform, judge competitions, and hold clinics and seminars. The festival also publishes a *National Directory of Female Jazz Performers*. These activities seem to be serving notice that women jazz musicians mean to survive and be heard.

AMATEUR PARTICIPATION: JAZZ EDUCATION

An investigation of jazz education in America today reveals many positive attributes. Colleges, high schools, junior high schools, and even grade schools are turning out stage bands that play expertly. High school stage bands have given amazing performances at festivals, and many college bands perform at a phenomenally high level of professionalism. Some colleges and universities regularly produce top-quality jazz ensembles, equal to the finest professional groups. These bands make worldwide tours, record superlative albums frequently including imaginative student scores, are reviewed favorably by the most prestigious jazz critics, and are recruited by well-known band leaders for full-time employment. After graduation some college players join such groups as Woody Herman, Maynard Ferguson, or Buddy Rich. Others become studio musicians or join professional house bands in Las Vegas. Many become music teachers, passing jazz expertise along to their students.

Of course, there are weaknesses in school jazz programs, mostly because of financial problems. Many public school music programs are not able to give the students any combo experience or any real knowledge of styles, literature, or artist-performers, and, most crucially, many students receive little or poor instruction in improvisation. In fact, the weakest factor in a high school stage band's performance is likely to be the improvised solos. Conservatories and universities that offer degrees in jazz must confront these deficiencies and make instruction in these skills mandatory. Often, the high school cannot do so. Fortunately, the National Association of Jazz Educators is aware of these educational needs, urges its membership to address them, and offers strategies for teaching them in the school jazz program.

There is little doubt that public school and college jazz band programs are thriving, expanding, and offering more jazz performance opportunities to more students than was ever dreamed of when the idea was initially conceived.

For Suggested Records, Suggestions for Listening, and Suggested Further Readings, see chapter 3.

THE INVENTION OF JAZZ

COMPONENTS FOR THE INVENTION OF JAZZ

How exactly did jazz come about? Without becoming entangled in too many historical details, it can be stated that when it was initially conceived, jazz was a new kind of musical expression that combined the characteristics of two cultures, European and African. (The label "European" is used to describe the state of American music at the beginning of the twentieth century. American composers, teachers, and musicians were using almost exclusively the 200-year-old principles of European harmony, chord types, melody, and form. All were imported from Europe, and there was as yet no indigenous American musical style.) Each of these two cultures contributed distinctive components.

BORROWED FROM EUROPEAN MUSICAL CULTURE

1. *Harmony:* the use of traditional European chord structures for melody support, the use of the European tonal system, the tempered scale, the strong sense of tonal center, and the process of chords progressing toward the tonal center.
2. *Forms:* the use of symmetrical 4-bar or 8-bar phrases, the use of antecedent and consequent phrases, the use of two-part and three-part compositions, and the nearly exclusive use of duple meters such as $\frac{2}{4}$ or $\frac{4}{4}$.

11

3. *Instrumentation:* the use of European instruments such as the saxophone, clarinet, cornet, trombone, tuba, piano, guitar, and string bass. (The banjo was newly invented in the United States but is said to have Arabic ancestors.)

BORROWED FROM AFRICAN MUSICAL CULTURE

1. *Melodic expressiveness:* the vocal tradition of bending pitches adopted for instrumental technique, and a variety of vocal inflections and tonal colors transferred to instrumental techniques.
2. *Improvisation:* the use of improvisational techniques and variational techniques as an important part of a presentation, the use of collective improvisation among several performers simultaneously (the Dixieland ensemble), and the spontaneous construction of the form of a given presentation.
3. *Syncopation:* the introduction into American popular music of the subtle technique of intricate syncopated rhythms layered over a simple, steady pulse. (This often complex phenomenon was unobserved in American popular music prior to the invention of jazz.)

The European factors were fairly rigid and formal but contained useful organizational qualities. The African factors were flexible and spontaneous. The combining of the two influences produced this remarkable music called jazz. When it was first developed, the differences between jazz and traditional music were more remarked upon than the similarities.

Because jazz was invented in America and developed from American social circumstances, Americans claim it as theirs. It could not have happened in France or Mexico or China because the social and cultural climates would not have been the same. It could have been an artistic product only of America.

Jazz is a musical reflection of twentieth-century American attitudes:

1. It is a melting-pot kind of music that continuously fuses new ideas and materials with old.
2. It embraces newness and fads.
3. Its spirit is competitive, aggressive, confident, and, for the most part, unsentimental.
4. Its success is often measured by commercial and popular appeal.
5. It is financially self-supporting and competes in the marketplace for its survival.

6. Its clarity and drive are uniquely American, partly because it is played with a predominance of wind instruments, not strings. (The saxophone, a woodwind mechanism in a brass body invented in Europe late in the nineteenth century and itself a *fusion* instrument, is a major American musical voice.)

SOME IMPORTANT
BLACK AMERICAN CONTRIBUTIONS

Jazz speaks to many black Americans in a very personal way because many elements of jazz structure are drawn from the black American experience. Some of these elements are the blues form, the blues scale, call and response, steady fundamental pulse combined with syncopated rhythms, dance music, and instrumentation.

What is the black American experience? Simply stated, it is the brief but powerful history of black Americans from eighteenth-century slavery to today's cultural and economic struggles. This study is concerned with how their African heritage and their daily lives affected the music they made. (The reader is encouraged to see *The Music of Black Americans* by Eileen Southern for a detailed historical perspective.)

THE BLUES FORM

The *blues form* evolved in the black American experience from borrowed European-American church harmony. From this church harmony came simple chord structures, an emphasis on the "amen" chord progression, and symmetrical 4-bar phrasing. Combined with these elements was the African talent for improvised melody.

The blues form in its most simple and uncomplicated state is a set of chords placed in twelve measures of musical time (see figure 3.1).

This set of chords is repeated several times in the course of blues performance. Note that the progression of chords is unlike that of chord progressions in the European tradition. The chords in measures 6 and 7 and in measures 10 and 11 (B♭ to F) make up a chordal sound known in the European tradition as the *plagal cadence*. It is also called the "amen" cadence and functions as a terminal sound at the ends of hymns. In the blues these chords are not found at the end

FIGURE 3.1.

but are structural centers of the form. Notice also that the C^7 chord for measure 9 would, if used in its traditional function, move to an F chord. Movement from C^7 to F is the most fundamental harmonic sound in European chord use. The C^7 is used here not to generate the F chord but instead as a link between F and B♭ (measures 8, 9, and 10). This is all contrary to the mainstream of eighteenth- and nineteenth-century European harmonic concepts.

One can also notice that there is no fixed melody. Instrumentalists improvise melody over the chord progression. There are some traditional blues songs with fixed melodies, but even these are more often than not altered each time the song is performed.

This form, known as the *blues progression,* has become more sophisticated over the years through the use of chord additions, chord substitutions, and chord alterations, but it is still essentially true to its origins and jazz musicians are still challenged to play it well.

Figure 3.2 is a more modern version of the 12-bar blues chord progression. It is more more modulatory (wandering from the home

FIGURE 3.2.

FIGURE 3.3.

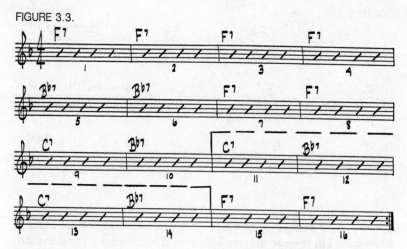

key into other temporary key centers) and contains more chords per measure, but it is at the same time similar to figure 3.1 in several respects. It seems to be set up in three 4-bar phrases as was the original, it begins with the major chord of the key it is in (in this case C), and the blues-quality IV chord (the chord built on the fourth degree of the C scale) is in place in measure 5 as it was in the original blues progression.

For the foregoing reasons this example is readily identifiable as 12-bar blues. Because of the additional chords per measure and the fact that these chords are used to create a modulatory effect, it can be identified as a more modern interpretation of 12-bar blues.

A frequently used variant of 12-bar blues is the format known as 16-bar blues. "Watermelon Man" is 16-bar blues. Figure 3.3 is a simple 16-bar blues chord progression. If figure 3.3 is compared to the first blues example (figure 3.1), it sounds almost exactly the same except for the bracketed material (measures 11, 12, 13, and 14), which has been added. Furthermore, measures 11 and 12 are a repeat of measures 9 and 10, and measures 13 and 14 are a second repeat. Thus, the additional measures are obtained by repetition.

If the second phrase is omitted from figure 3.1 (measures 5, 6, 7, and 8) and there is direct movement from measure 4 to measure 9, another common variant known as 8-bar blues is obtained.

Still another common variant of the 12-bar blues progression is one in which the flavor of the chords has been changed from major to minor. This music is given the characteristic name of "minor blues." Figure 3.4 is an example:

FIGURE 3.4.

It is probably a conservative estimate that from sixty to seventy percent of all performed and recorded jazz compositions are blues or blues-based in their structure. This would mean that an understanding of the blues form is extremely important to the understanding of jazz in general.

THE BLUES SCALE

The *blues scale* evolved in the black American experience as a melodic pattern, written in Western notation, that could imply and function for some of the African vocal improvisatory devices. It enables the jazz improviser to create the blues quality in melodic terms so that it may be expressed on a solo trumpet, guitar, saxophone, or some other melodic instrument. Figure 3.5 is the basic form of the blues scale:

FIGURE 3.5.

These tones, when used in various combinations, can make small melodic gestures that express the blues quality. Figure 3.6 provides three examples.

FIGURE 3.6.

16

Figure 3.7 is a melody composed of only tones from the blues scale, with the scale built on C.

FIGURE 3.7.

In actual practice the blues scale is not often used in its pure state (as in figure 3.7). Most players and writers use the pure blues scale as a basis but add extra tones to it whenever they choose. Figure 3.8 is the same blues scale with arrows denoting additional tones that will make it more flexible for the improviser.

FIGURE 3.8.

Knowledge of the blues scale and the ability to use it are essential for any jazz musician. It is a necessary tool for the improviser, and it is used to express non-blues music as well.

CALL AND RESPONSE

The device of *call and response* is commonly found in the work songs of field workers and laboring crews and in the congregational singing of black church music. The leader sings a phrase of the song and the group responds by echoing the phrase exactly or with some modifications (see figure 3.9). This type of group singing is common in African music. Sometimes the leader "tells a story" one phrase at a time, with the responsorial group echoing each phrase in rhythm, and sometimes the group replies with a refrain which is the same each time. This all takes place within the framework of a steady tempo.

When this technique was transferred to the instrumental ensemble, the soloist functioned as the leader and the saxophones,

FIGURE 3.9.

trumpets, and trombones became the responsorial group. The soloist usually performed improvisatory statements while the ensemble played fixed melodic clichés known as *riffs*. This technique works quite well within the blues format.

STEADY PULSE AND SYNCOPATION

Steady pulse and syncopation form a common effect in African drum and instrumental ensembles, and because improvising is so important in the jazz scheme this effect became a normal quality in jazz performance.

The easiest way to grasp this concept is to listen to recordings of authentic African drum ensembles. (See Suggested Records at the end of this chapter.) In many such presentations there is a steady, unflagging pulse and layered over the steady pulse is a complex of other rhythms. These other rhythms come and go and are at times more prominent, at other times less prominent. They are involved less with the fundamental steady accents of the regular pulse and are concerned more with *syncopation,* the accenting or stressing of what the listener expects to be a weak portion of the rhythm. The same kind of rhythmic thinking appears in the jazz ensemble (see Rhythmic Complex in chapter 6) where a drummer may establish the fundamental pulse rhythm while the bassist performs an ornamented version of this pulse, the pianist hits chords in another rhythm, the ensemble chords in still another rhythm, and, finally, the soloist improvises with more contrasting rhythms. This is a common situation in jazz ensembles of all sizes and is a contributing factor to the jazz feeling of any presentation.

The group is collectively improvising many different rhythms and the effect evolved naturally as jazz was developed by black Americans.

DANCE MUSIC

In many African ceremonial performances, music and dance are equal partners. The evolution of social dancing in America was influenced by the black American experience involving jazz as the accompanying music. This was particularly true of jazz in its formative years. Jazz was dance music from its crude beginnings up to the 1940s. Then, with the appearance of jazz clubs where people sat and listened, this began to change. Now, jazz concerts and jazz clubs (without dance floors) provide normal outlets for jazz musicians. And all jazz players know that a more intense type of improvising is required for listening than for dancing. Concessions that formerly were made to dancers, such as danceable tempos, recognizable melodies, steady pulse, and modest lengths, are no longer so important. Interesting, creative improvisation has become the most important factor.

JAZZ INSTRUMENTATION

The black American experience helped to dictate the specific instruments used for jazz performance. Why did the early jazz players choose an instrumentation consisting of clarinets, cornets, trombones, and, of course, drums?

At the turn of the century, the American air was filled with band music. There were military bands, concert bands, civic bands, neighborhood bands, fraternal club bands, boys' bands, professional touring bands, theater bands, circus bands, outdoor band concerts, and parades for all occasions. These were the instrumental ensembles which black Americans most often heard, and so early jazz players were easily attracted to clarinets, cornets, trombones, and drums. These were also the most available instruments; after World War I, the U.S. Army dismantled its large military band system and army surplus musical instruments were plentiful and inexpensive.

Other reasons for choosing these instruments were that they were portable in size and shape and were less likely to be damaged by outdoor use and weather than were violins, violas, cellos, oboes, bassoons, etc. They could also produce more power than string instruments. The saxophone, which was added to the jazz ensemble at a later time, was also originally a band instrument and it fit the jazz players' requirements nicely.

19

Originally, jazz was exclusively a black American musical genre, but exclusivity is no longer possible. Today, the advanced state of electronic science and the easy transmission of music make jazz available to musicians anywhere in the world. Anyone may imitate it faithfully, assimilate it, and embrace it as one's own means of musical expression. It is impossible most of the time to determine by listening alone if a performance is being played by a black American, a white American, a German, a Japanese, a South American, or a representative of any other nationality or race. Some may consider this development to be a ripoff of black music, but it is primarily a by-product of modern technology and cannot be controlled by any person or group.

As has been stated before, however, the formative roots of jazz spring from black American musicians, and the innovators continue to be mostly black Americans.

SUGGESTED RECORDS:

IRAKERE, *Irakere*. Columbia JC-35655
GATO BARBIERI, *Bolivia*. Flying Dutchman 10158
ELVIN JONES, *The Main Force*. Vanguard VSD-79372
JOANNE BRACKEEN, *Tring-a-ling*. Choice CRS-1016
GENE AMMONS, *Got My Own*. Prestige 10058
ART BLAKEY, *Buhaina*. Prestige 10067
FREDDIE HUBBARD, *Red Clay*. CTI 6001
WOODY SHAW, *Moontrane*. Muse 5058
DIZZY GILLESPIE, *The Dizzie Gillespie Big 7 at the Montreux Jazz Festival, 1975*. Pablo 2310-749
African and Afro-American Drums. Folkways 4502

SUGGESTIONS FOR LISTENING:

1. Which recordings reflect the blues form? The blues scale?
2. Which recordings contain call and response?
3. Which jazz recording most accurately reflects the African drums recording with regard to steady pulse vs. syncopation?
4. Which U.S. recordings purposely use African source materials?
5. Which recordings represent non-American musicians?

6. Which recording uses the most elaborate arranging/composing techniques?

SUGGESTED FURTHER READINGS:

The Jazz Life, Nat Hentoff; chapters 2, 3, 5, 11.
Jazz Styles, Mark C. Gridley; chapter 19.
Jazz: A History, Frank Tirro; chapters 1, 2, 3.
Jazz City, Leroy Ostransky; chapters 1 and 2.
Hear Me Talkin' to Ya, Nat Shapiro and Nat Hentoff, eds.; chapter 21.
The Music of Black Americans, Eileen Southern; parts I and II.

THE LIFE

The life of a jazz musician is demanding, and artistic integrity is often at odds with cold and realistic business deals. The two spheres must meet on a common ground and compromises must be made. A successful jazz artist is part showman, part gypsy, part artist, part recording engineer, and part manager. Some juggle all of this with ease, are sustained by personalities that can withstand the tensions, and are always in demand for performances and recordings. Clark Terry, Dizzy Gillespie, Ray Brown, and Oscar Peterson, just to name a few, have never been out of the center of jazz activities, have never had health or emotional problems, and work as often as they wish.

The life has attractions: After moderate success, one may expect applause, publicity, concert reviews, record reviews, adulation and acclaim, autographs, interviews, seeing one's name in lights, and more.

The life has temptations: Ego trips, temperamental excesses, self-delusion, and self indulgence, any of which may lead to a dependence on alcohol or drugs. These in turn bring on personal or legal troubles.

The life is mainly nocturnal and is spent in such locations as clubs, bars, lounges, restaurants, auditoriums, concert halls, outdoor stages, theaters, recording studios, TV studios, and film studios. Usually, one is not permanently located but instead is constantly traveling by car, bus, train, or plane, living out of one's luggage, sleeping and eating on an irregular schedule. Duke Ellington and Woody Herman thrived on travel, and being on the road became their life. Others never adjust to the constant traveling and find that a feeling of rootlessness affects their work.

The nightclubs are, unfortunately, too often owned and inhabited by shady people involved in any illegal enterprises that are profitable. Thus, the vices are too available and too commonplace for the gullible performer to ignore or refuse. Regardless of how fans may perceive them, jazz artists are sometimes naive, immature, and insecure. Additionally, a jazz musician's background is often that of small-town life or the urban ghetto. Sudden success or imitation of one's idols are conducive to excessive sampling of all of the deliciously wicked and costly temptations, including hard drugs. This error can be the beginning of a hellish life.

The jazz life can deliver exhilarating highs and contrastingly boring, depressing lows. A superior personal performance followed by congratulations from colleagues is a high. The tedium of travel, a poor review, or dissatisfaction with one's performance are lows. These extremes test one's emotional stability, and some performers turn to dubious crutches for support and serenity. The drug problems of entertainers and jazz musicians have always received a disproportionate amount of attention from the media. Although it is certainly true that drug addiction is not uncommon among other segments of society, the fact remains that performing artists, perhaps because of the stresses of the lifestyle, have been particularly susceptible to this pitfall.

One hopeful word regarding the drug horror: There seems to be a lessening of drug use by jazz musicians. This is partly because there has been more drug education lately, and young people are taking advantage of it. It is also partly because young jazz musicians are generally better educated than ever before. They are more health-conscious and more aware of the tragic consequences of drug abuse.

ATTITUDES

The classically trained musician displays an attitude of reverence toward the music he or she performs. The masters such as Bach, Mozart, and Beethoven are placed on a pedestal, and their music is treated with great respect as "serious" music. It may be interpreted by conductors and performers, but it is seldom tampered with structurally. Tempos and dynamics may be altered, an obligatory repeat of a section may be ignored, or a shift of emphasis may bring out a hitherto obscure bit of texture or countermelody. Beyond these interpretative alterations, the master's intentions are respected. By contrast, the jazz musician seems to display an irreverent attitude toward the music used as a basis for his or her performance. Certainly, the jazz artist admires Cole Porter or Duke Ellington or George Gershwin as composers, but jazz demands that their music be played not as it appears on the published page but as the performer conceives it anew. The original compositions are merely outlines for the player's improvisational skills.

Largely because of this attitude of irreverence toward the music on the printed page, jazz appears to the classically trained performer to be an informal, casual, social music. On the surface, this is true. The environment in which jazz is so often performed helps to create this impression. A nightclub, lounge, or bar atmosphere is anything but formal, and the jazz musician's creative struggle takes place in such arenas. The concert hall atmosphere is a traditionally formal environment, and the music-making process there is normally one of deep seriousness. In the cabaret or nightclub, people are having fun. Glasses tinkle, dishes rattle, there is conversation and laughter, and the jazz musician creates within this setting. But make no mistake— the jazz artist is no less serious about his or her music than is the classically trained musician.

Along with the informal attitude, a special insider's language— a slangy, humorous language with code words—has developed. Much of this language is invented by black musicians, passed on to white musicians, and eventually words such as "dig," "square," "gig," "cats," "chicks," "cool," "groovy," and "bread" enter the mainstream of American vernacular.

Another reason for the attitude of irreverence toward the music they play is that jazz musicians are by and large not restricted by a sense of nostalgia for the past. Ragtime, Dixieland, swing, and so on are little more than curiosities to most of them, especially the younger ones. For the majority, the older styles are music history; their energies are directed toward newness, innovation, and further explorations of the idiom. The idea that pieces of music are untouchable classics is foreign to the thought processes of a progressive jazz musician. It is also true that, for a working jazz musician, newness is important for the commercial aspects of his or her craft.

Attitudes vary among different age groups of jazz players. The older and sometimes unschooled players are often not at all innovative. They found their style of playing long ago and it is the only way they will play. They are not interested in new ideas and will not attempt to play or even listen to much new music. If they have sufficient status they may continue to record and perform without any changes in their playing styles. Contrary to this generality, other older players may be young at heart and may listen to and try new ideas. Their playing styles are not fixed for all time but continue to change and grow.

The younger generations of players are, for the most part, better trained and more innovative. Many of them have college degrees in music, listen to the new players and styles, and have worked in a variety of pop and jazz idioms. Some have progressed from rock to jazz. Some have studied with professional instrumentalists, and some have worked with well-known bands and combos. Their playing is generally more flexible and refreshing—often astonishingly so.

Jazz players are usually at their best when playing in comfortable, sympathetic surroundings. For example, there are those who play best when they can "showboat" on a stage in a concert atmosphere. Lionel Hampton, Dizzy Gillespie, and Buddy Rich are examples. Others play best in an intimate club atmosphere, and there are many who fit into this category. Finally, there are those who do their best work in the recording studio. John Klemmer, Tom Scott, and Miles Davis exemplify this type of jazz player.

PAYING DUES

The expression "paying dues" is one of those jazz slang phrases that has been adopted by nonmusicians. What exactly does it mean?

For professional jazz musicians, paying dues means going through all the learning steps and devoting all the time needed to acquire the necessary skills to do their jobs well. And so the professionals who have paid their dues have studied with several good teachers to learn the basic mechanics of how to play their instruments properly. They have also played all types of music professionally for pay. This means weddings, bar mitzvahs, parties and receptions of all kinds, dances, conventions, beauty pageants, shows of all descriptions, and many other types of commercial music. They have also made a special study of jazz and jazz playing. This means listening to live and recorded jazz players and analyzing their techniques. It also means learning jazz literature and memorizing jazz and pop tunes that might be performed in a jazz context. And, further, they must have practiced playing jazz every day so that all of their expressive faculties are centered on creative jazz musicianship. Finally, they must have participated as often as possible in playing sessions with many different groups and players, so that they have developed a feeling for playing jazz competitively. This is called "sitting in." An excellent way to advance one's jazz playing concepts is to attempt to stick it out and play with musicians who are more skilled and more experienced, so the conscientious jazz student discovers where the jam sessions are and gets into them as often as possible. These sessions are the best of all learning experiences.

There are no overnight shortcuts to mastering these skills. Success can be achieved only hour by hour, day by day, year by year in an accumulative, systematic fashion. This is what most musicians would call paying their dues.

Some also consider the following as part of the process of paying dues: playing circuses and carnivals in the mud; playing parades in the rain or snow; being cheated by leaders, managers, and agents; backing up poor singers and dancers who blame the musicians for their own mistakes; trying to read dog-eared, water-spotted, poorly copied music manuscript in near total darkness; having one's instruments stolen; being unable to afford needed instrument repairs; having to put up with drunks, addicts, and crazies; driving a cab or clerking in a store in order to eat; being asked by a segment of the public to play for free; being discriminated against because of color, sex, or profession; and on and on and on. Dues are paid in many different ways.

VERSATILITY

Successful extensions of their musical careers are achieved by many performers. Aside from being fine players, quite a few become prominent composers, arrangers, conductors, producers, publishers, authors, song writers, educators, critics, and experienced voices in various facets of the music business. Here are some examples:

• *Tom Scott* is one of those extremely talented but anonymous studio session performers whose abilities make an album come alive.

Being the son of a studio musician, he has grown up in the familiar environs of the electronic recording studio. He is a woodwind specialist who plays all the saxophones, clarinets, and flutes. His soloing has been heard behind Joni Mitchell, Carole King, Ray Charles, the Fifth Dimension, Barbra Streisand, and Sergio Mendes, just to name a few. In addition to leading his own jazz-rock group, the L.A. Express, which records frequently, he is also a facile arranger/composer and can be called in at the last minute to redo arrangements for an album deadline. Performer, arranger, leader, and director—he does it all, and as evidence, he owns Grammy nominations and "Most Valuable Player" citations by the National Academy of Recording Arts and Sciences.

• *Ralph Burns* was a jazz pianist with Charlie Barnet, Red Norvo, and Woody Herman. He became known as an arranger and composer while with Herman, and he now orchestrates Broadway shows such as *Cabaret* and *Chicago* and composes scores for TV specials and films.

• *Elliot Lawrence* was the pianist-leader of a college band at the University of Pennsylvania. He scored arrangements for the group and later scored for a radio house band. This band went to New York and recorded for Columbia, becoming an overnight sensation. He now scores for TV and films, conducts recording sessions, and is a musical director for TV specials.

• *Quincy Jones* played trumpet with Count Basie and Lionel Hampton, studied music in Boston, and became a free-lance arranger in New York, where he scored for the Ray Anthony band. Using this experience, he began to write for recording sessions and then went to Hollywood and became a well-known film composer.

Film scoring was a powerful attraction for other jazz-oriented players such as Oliver Nelson (alto sax), J. J. Johnson (trombone), and Don Ellis (trumpet), all of whom have used their jazz backgrounds to good advantage.

These people and others have become successful because they are multidimensional and versatile. Besides being skilled performers, they can conduct, arrange, compose, and produce a product on demand in the world of commercial music. Their backgrounds as jazz performers were the springboards to their present positions.

The jazz life may be lucrative, pleasurable, and creative—or it may be paltry, anxious, and sordid. It depends on several factors: the person's background, training, personality, and talent; the particular circumstances which frame each day's events; and how he or she manages those circumstances to the best advantage—in other words, capitalizing on the breaks.

For Suggested Records, Suggestions for Listening, and Suggested Further Readings, see chapter 5.

THE LISTENERS

There are many people on this ever-shrinking globe who take light music seriously. They know and love and are connoisseurs of popular music; it is the only type of music that holds their interest. It speaks to them, moves them, and gratifies their musical desires. For some, popular music is the only music to which they have ever been exposed. Others have heard the symphony, the opera, and various other types of concert music, and although they understand it well enough, it is not the music they most enjoy. These music fans pay for and listen to pop singers and instrumentalists, show music from the Broadway stage, and jazz.

Since the development of the communications satellite and the transistor radio, the influence of recorded American popular music is heard even in the most remote and isolated areas of the world. Wherever the traveler may go, American or American-style pop music is there if a radio is present.

All the world loves American jazz. There are serious jazz fans and record collectors in every European country and behind the Iron Curtain. There have been jazz clubs and record collectors in England and France since the 1920s. The Japanese love jazz and fill huge auditoriums with polite, adoring fans to hear American jazz concerts. Third World countries in South America and Africa appreciate jazz and recognize many similarities between jazz and their native musics. Wherever U.S. jazz ambassadors travel on State Department tours, they are welcomed and respected as artists.

There is much space devoted to jazz in foreign journals, periodicals, and newspapers. In Europe an American jazz concert is as important as a symphony concert or an opera. There are quite a few magazines in Europe and America specializing in jazz interviews, articles, and reviews. Some of these are: *Coda*, Ontario, Canada; *Crescendo*, Williston Park, New York; *Down Beat*, Chicago, Illinois; *Cadence*, Redwood, New York; *Jazz Magazine*, Northport, New York; *Jazz Journal International*, London, England; *Journal of Jazz Studies*, Rutgers University, New Jersey; *Radio Free Jazz*, Washington, D.C.; *N.A.J.E. Educator*, Manhattan, Kansas. The last-mentioned journal is published by the National Association of Jazz Educators, an organization of public school and college jazz educators. There are also publications produced by jazz record dealers and discography compilers. Many radio stations specialize in jazz, and there are some twenty-four-hour jazz stations. Public TV periodically broadcasts jazz specials which bring jazz and jazz musicians to a larger American audience, without commercials.

The reader is encouraged to see *Serious Music—And All That Jazz!* by Henry Pleasants, wherein the author quite logically and clearly forecasts what he terms "the Afro-American epoch." He contends that future musicologists will see a great part of the twentieth century as such an epoch and the impact of most of the world's twentieth-century "serious" composers as comparatively insignificant.

Colleges and universities, after sixty or seventy years of neglect, have begun to pay serious attention to jazz, one of America's most unique and precious resources. Earnest study, research, and development of jazz is at last beginning to take place on college campuses. All of this interest, both new and renewed, means that someone is listening. What do listeners hear and enjoy in jazz?

A rock show is a visual experience with lights, costumes, makeup, explosions, etc. With jazz, the spectacle is superfluous. The amateur reviewer of a jazz presentation mistakenly writes about what was seen instead of what was heard. Jazz is not only predominantly aural but it also requires an informed, intellectual kind of listening. This is probably why some jazz journalists call jazz the classical aspect of popular music—it requires an educated listener to appreciate it.

Jazz is not always a comforting, easy-listening kind of music. Sometimes it is a disturbing, irritating, shrill statement that is both emotive and intellectual—emotive in the expressiveness of the solo performer and intellectual in the improvisational treatment of the initial musical premise.

Jazz performers are very competitive and often try to outdo each other as they play. The informed listener knows this and listens for it. He or she knows about "cutting sessions," using the other player's "licks" (ideas) and the use of "steals" (quotes). When a player is bested by another, the jazz buff recognizes the event. When a player is not trying, just going through the motions, playing clichés, and coasting, the discerning listener knows. When a player does something effective, clever, witty, or soulful, the listeners respond with applause or audible remarks.

Many jazz lovers have come from high schools and colleges, from the ranks of former rock fans who are no longer stimulated by rock music. They have become more perceptive listeners, have learned to recognize certain players by sound and style, and are familiar with some general jazz styles; they have learned to understand competitiveness among players and the art of the improviser.

SUGGESTED RECORDS:

MILES DAVIS, *Water Babies*. Columbia PC-34396
JACK WILKINS, *Merge*. Chiaroscuro CR-156
CLARE FISCHER, *Easy Livin'*. Revelation 2
JIM HALL/RON CARTER, *Alone Together*. Milestone MSP-9045
HUBERT LAWS, *Carnegie Hall*. CTI 6025
CANNONBALL ADDERLY, *Inside Straight*. Fantasy F-9435
BRECKER BROTHERS, *Back to Back*. Arista AL-4061
DEXTER GORDON, *Homecoming*. Columbia PG-34650

SUGGESTIONS FOR LISTENING:

1. Which recordings will appeal to the rock-oriented listener? Why?
2. Which recordings will appeal to the mainstream jazz listener? Why?
3. Which recordings will appeal to the traditional jazz fan? Why?
4. Which recordings will appeal to the classically oriented fan? Why?
5. Which recordings are funky or emotive in character?
6. Which recordings are cool or remote in character?

SUGGESTED FURTHER READINGS:

The Jazz Story, Dave Dexter Jr.; chapter 12.
Jazz City, Leroy Ostransky; chapter 10.
The Jazz Life, Nat Hentoff; Introduction, chapters 6 and 8.
Jazz Styles, Mark C. Gridley; chapter 20.
The Story of Jazz, Marshall W. Stearns; chapter 24.
Serious Music—And All That Jazz!, Henry Pleasants.

CHAPTER SIX

THE ORGANIZATION OF JAZZ MATERIALS

The organizational systems that make up jazz are varied and diverse but all converge to contribute to its unique character. The list of organizational systems includes the literature (the American pop idiom), the instrumentation, instrumental roles, forms (the arranger), the rhythmic complex, styles, and the process of self-renewal.

THE LITERATURE

One of the most important organizational elements in jazz is the music literature it uses as a basis. Jazz most often uses music that is identifiable as belonging to the American popular music idiom. Thus, jazz musicians may play music from the Broadway musical stage, movie themes, top 40 songs and tunes from the pop charts, old standards, folk songs, symphony themes, and many other types of music churned out by pop and commercial music composers. Jazz players also compose original tunes, however, and not all the music they use is borrowed from other sources. Some examples of original jazz tunes would be "Moment's Notice" by John Coltrane, "Night in Tunisia" by Dizzy Gillespie, "Airegin" by Sonny Rollins, " 'Round Midnight" by Thelonios Monk, and "Stolen Moments" by Oliver Nelson. Even though jazz composition has become more common in the last several decades, the use of current pop material coexists with the new jazz tunes and, more importantly, the newly composed jazz tunes contain chords, chord progressions, and melodic ideas that spring from the general pop idiom.

THE AMERICAN POP IDIOM

What is the American popular music idiom? When jazz first came into existence as a form of musical expression, the musicians used the American popular idiom of the day—marches, polkas, waltzes, work songs, theater songs, barroom ballads, bordello songs, spirituals, sentimental parlor ballads, revival songs, etc.—as a basis for jazz expression. The use of the popular song continued in each decade, and it is still a valid practice today.

From the 1920s to the early 1950s, the American popular song was a thriving business, supplying dance bands and their singers, radio and recording orchestras and their singers, Broadway musicals, and movie studios with a continuous stream of new songs. Nearly the entire pop song business was at one time centered in a few office buildings in Manhattan, known as "Tin Pan Alley." One example of an unqualified success in this tough business is Irving Berlin. Either "White Christmas" or "God Bless America" alone could have made him a wealthy man.

Conversely, the quality of many of both yesterday's and today's songs is often poor, and many hacks survive and make a living with second-rate material. But talented song composers have always been able to produce artistic gems. These often become evergreens, and they continue to be used long after their initial publication. Jazz musicians contribute to the evergreen status by continuing to perform, arrange, and record certain songs which, because of their melody and harmony, are interesting to play. Some evergreens are still attractive to jazz musicians forty or fifty years after their first publication.

The broad spectrum of the American pop idiom encompasses music with Cuban, Brazilian, Caribbean, and Mexican flavors as well as gospel, rock, country and western, bluegrass, urban blues, country blues, and many more regional influences. There are differences, of course, but there are also many common elements. A look at the title groupings that follow might aid in discovering common properties:

U.S. CITIES OR STATES IN TITLES

"Goin' Back to Houston"
"St. Louis Blues"
"Autumn in New York"
"Moonlight in Vermont"
"Old Cape Cod"
"Jersey Bounce"
"On the Boardwalk in Atlantic City"
"Oklahoma"
"Do You Know the Way to San Jose?"
"California Here I Come"
"I Left My Heart in San Francisco"
"Wichita Lineman"
"By the Time I Get to Phoenix"
"Moon over Miami"
"Back Home Again in Indiana"
"I Got a Gal in Kalamazoo"
"Pennsylvania Polka"
"Rainy Night in Georgia"
"Georgia on My Mind"
"Hooray for Hollywood"
"Chicago"
"Yellow Rose of Texas"
"Stars Fell on Alabama"
"Kansas City"
"Carolina in the Morning"
"Do You Know What It Means to Miss New Orleans?"
"Nevada"
"Big D"
"Mississippi Mud"
"Down by the O-hi-o"
"Poor Little Rhode Island"
"Manhattan"
"Just a Little Bit South of North Carolina"
"Louisiana Hayride"
"Deep in the Heart of Texas"
"New York State of Mind"

WEATHER TITLES

"Rainy Days and Mondays"
"Soon It's Gonna Rain"
"Into Each Life Some Rain Must Fall"
"Stormy Weather"
"September in the Rain"
"April Showers"
"With the Wind and the Rain in Your Hair"

"Singin' in the Rain"
"Come Rain or Come Shine"
"Raindrops Keep Fallin' on My Head"
"Here's That Rainy Day"
"Don't Rain on My Parade"
"Rainy Night in Rio"
"Till the Clouds Roll By"
"Let the Sun Shine In"
"On a Clear Day"
"Sunny Side of the Street"
"Having a Heat Wave"
"Too Darned Hot"
"High on a Windy Hill"
"Gone with the Wind"
"Foggy Day in London Town"
"Winter Wonderland"
"Let It Snow"
"Baby, It's Cold Outside"
"When the Sun Comes Out"

MONTH OR SEASON TITLES

"Autumn in New York"
"Autumn Leaves"
"Early Autumn"
" 'Tis Autumn"
"Indian Summer"
"September Song"
"September in the Rain"
"Lost April"
"April in Paris"
"April Showers"
"I'll Remember April"
"Spring Is Here"
"Love Turns Winter into Spring"
"It Might as Well Be Spring"
"Spring Will Be a Little Late This Year"
"The Isle of May"
"June in January"
"June Is Bustin' Out All Over"
"Summertime"
"The Summer Knows"

"BLUE" IN TITLES

"Blue Skies"
"Serenade in Blue"
"Blue Moon"

"My Blue Heaven"
"Birth of the Blues"
"I've Got a Right to Sing the Blues"
"St. Louis Blues"
"Little Girl Blue"
"Blues in the Night"
"Am I Blue?"
"When the Blue of the Night"
"Blue Room"
"Basin Street Blues"
"Beyond the Blue Horizon"
"Blue Hawaii"
"Blue Tango"
"Blue Champagne"
"Under a Blanket of Blue"
"When Sunny Gets Blue"
"Love Is Blue"
"Alice Blue Gown"
"In the Blue of Evening"

OTHER COLORS IN TITLES

"Red Sails in the Sunset"
"Deep Purple"
"Green Eyes"
"Yellow Rose of Texas"
"Tie a Yellow Ribbon"
"Yellow Days"
"Pink Champagne"
"Rose Room"
"Red Roses for a Blue Lady"
"Look for the Silver Lining"
"Scarlet Ribbons"
"My Little Brown Book"
"Blue, Green, Grey and Gone"
"That Old Black Magic"
"Green Dolphin Street"
"Evergreen"
"Bye, Bye, Blackbird"

"MOON" IN TITLES

"Racing with the Moon"
"Blue Moon"
"Moonlight in Vermont"
"Moon over Miami"
"Carolina Moon"
"Moonglow"

"How High the Moon"
"Moonlight Cocktail"
"Moon River"
"Chapel in the Moonlight"
"Moonlight Becomes You"
"Moonlight and Shadows"
"When the Moon Comes over the Mountain"
"Orchids in the Moonlight"
"Full Moon and Empty Arms"
"Harvest Moon"
"That Old Devil Moon"
"Moon Love"
"By the Light of the Silvery Moon"
"On Moonlight Bay"
"Polka Dots and Moonbeams"
"Paper Moon"

FEMALE NAME IN TITLES

"Marie"
"Maria"
"Charmaine"
"Louise"
"Louisa"
"Sweet Sue"
"Laura"
"Hello Dolly"
"Mame"
"Sweet Georgia Brown"
"Liza"
"I'm Coming Virginia"
"Sweet Lorraine"
"Mandy"
"Stella by Starlight"
"Josephine"
"Peg o' My Heart"
"Jean"
"Jeannine"
"Ramona"
"Dolores"
"Tangerine"
"Chloe"
"Nola"
"Once in Love with Amy"
"Portrait of Jenny"
"Michelle"
"Tammy"
"Ida"
"Dinah"

"Margie"
"Nancy with the Laughing Face"
"Rosalie"
"Gigi"
"Georgie Girl"
"Proud Mary"
"Sunny"
"Second-Hand Rose"

MALE NAME IN TITLES

"Happiness Is Just a Thing Called Joe"
"Joey"
"I'm Just Wild about Harry"
"Just My Bill"
"Alexander's Ragtime Band"
"Oh, Johnny"
"Bill Bailey"
"Roger Young"
"Sam, You Made the Pants Too Long"
"Mack the Knife"
"Leroy Brown"
"Open the Door, Richard"
"Rudolph the Red-Nosed Reindeer"
"Alfie"
"Charlie My Boy"
"Johnny-One-Note"
"Danny Boy"

TIME OF DAY TITLES

"Night and Day"
"All through the Night"
"Tonight"
"In the Still of the Night"
"The Night Has a Thousand Eyes"
"The Night Is Young"
"Night Train"
"Saturday Night"
"The Way You Look Tonight"
"If I Could Be with You One Hour Tonight"
"You and the Night and the Music"
" 'Round Midnight"
"The Night Was Made for Love"
"Just the Way You Look Tonight"
"I Could Have Danced All Night"
"The Night We Called It a Day"
"Dancing in the Dark"
"In the Cool of the Evening"

"Some Enchanted Evening"
"At Sundown"
"Suppertime"
"When Day Is Done"
"Daybreak"
"Come Saturday Morning"
"Sunrise Serenade"
"Carolina in the Morning"
"Softly, as in a Morning Sunrise"
"A Lazy Afternoon"
"High Noon"

TRAVEL TITLES

"Route 66"
"Chattanooga Choo Choo"
"Atcheson, Topeka and the Santa Fe"
"Leavin' on a Jet Plane"
"By the Time I Get to Phoenix"
"Country Roads"
"Sentimental Journey"
"Lonesome Road"
"The Happy Wanderer"
"Take the 'A' Train"
"Trolley Song"
"Wagon Wheels"
"Around the World"
"Two for the Road"
"Slow Boat to China"
"My Ship"
"Let's Get away from It All"
"Flying down to Rio"
"Up, Up, and Away"
"Beyond the Blue Horizon"
"Homeward Bound"
"Get out of Town"
"Cruising down the River"

"STREET" IN TITLES

"Street of Dreams"
"Sunny Side of the Street"
"Easy Street"
"On the Street where You Live"
"Green Dolphin Street"
"Boulevard of Broken Dreams"
"Basin Street Blues"
"Forty-Second Street"
"Just a Little Street where Old Friends Meet"

OCCULT TITLES

"Ghost of a Chance"
"That Old Black Magic"
"It's Witchcraft"
"That Old Devil Moon"
"Voodoo Woman"
"Ghost Riders in the Sky"
"Love Your Magic Spell Is Everywhere"
"It's Magic"
"The Witch Doctor"
"Out of This World"
"You Stepped out of a Dream"

These lists have been assembled merely to provide some idea of the immensity of the subject. It should be emphasized that these groupings of songs are not at all comprehensive. Indeed, they are only the tip of the iceberg. The body of American song is an exceedingly large one, and a study of American popular songs in detail would require much further investigation.

One of the first general observations upon reading these title lists is that the public seems to prefer songs on the subjects of locales, rain, autumn, spring, blue, moon, night, and female names. To assemble lists of titles that contain the word "love" or the word "you" would have been formidable. Song writers have always known that these words are choice subjects for songs. But, more importantly, what similar musical properties do all these songs possess? They all contain:

1. Singable melody with supporting chords
2. Steady pulse
3. Melodic clichés and formulas
4. Harmonic clichés and formulas
5. Limited number of forms

Each of the properties listed above can be identified in thousands of popular songs:

1. They all have memorable melodies and, with the words, are easy for the listener to remember and sing (at least a key phrase or two).
2. The speed or tempo at which these songs move remains steady and does not fluctuate from slow to fast or vice versa.
3. There are well-used clichés that occur always in pop melody. These clichés contain common scale intervals and stereotyped contours and

FIGURE 6.1.

CONTOUR MODEL

MONA LISA

SOME ENCHANTED EVENING

I'LL BE HOME FOR CHRISTMAS

SMOKE GETS IN YOUR EYES

rhythms. Figure 6.1 is an example of reuse. Some other songs that begin with the same contour are "On the Alamo," "Near You," "With a Song in My Heart," and "(I) Can't Begin to Tell You."

Figure 6.2 is another example of reuse. Some other songs that begin with the same contour are "Everything I Have Is Yours," "Someone to Watch over Me," "P.S. I Love You," "Pretty Baby," "I Hear a Rhapsody," and "Do You Know What It Means to Miss New Orleans?"

4. Harmony clichés occur repeatedly in all pop songs. This means that particular chords are almost surely going to be followed by certain other chords. This practice produces a predictable and cohesive quality in the music. Rarely will the composer totally surprise the listener. Figures 6.3-6.10 are a few examples of chord progression formulas and harmony clichés used again and again in pop songs.

5. With few exceptions, pop songs have an outward shape that can be described as AABA, ABA, ABAC, ABCA, or some similar combina-

FIGURE 6.2.

CONTOUR MODEL

OUT OF NOWHERE

I'VE GROWN ACCUSTOMED TO HER FACE

BEGIN THE BEGUINE

IN A SENTIMENTAL MOOD

TENNESSEE WALTZ

tion of repetition and contrast. The letters stand for phrases of the song, with each phrase normally 8 measures in length. For a significant period of time in the 1930s, 1940s, and 1950s, the standard or most common form for a pop song was AABA, and the length was almost always 32 measures. The following combinations of A and B will illustrate the standard 32-bar song:

A An 8-measure phrase
A A repetition of the first phrase, but using different lyrics
B A contrasting 8-measure phrase (the *bridge*)
A A final 8-measure phrase like the first phrase or only slightly modified as a conclusion.

FIGURE 6.3.

FIGURE 6.4.

FIGURE 6.5.

FIGURE 6.6.

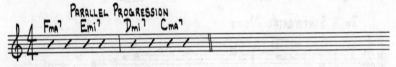

FIGURE 6.7.

FIGURE 6.8.

FIGURE 6.9.

FIGURE 6.10.

(THIS RHYTHM IS ALSO A CLICHÉ)

Here are some examples of tunes using these forms:

AABA "I Got Rhythm"
      " 'Round Midnight"
      "Body and Soul"

ABAC "How High the Moon"
      "Green Dolphin Street"
      "Here's That Rainy Day"

ABCD "Stella by Starlight"
      "My Funny Valentine"
      "Black Orpheus"

 ABA "I'll Remember April" (sixteen-measure phrases)

Each of the five listed properties will most likely be present if the song is to become a hit. The public must be able to assimilate the new song easily. Working within these limitations, the composer hopes to produce something original and enduring, and many times he or she succeeds. These songs then become attractive and useful to the jazz musician.

As was stated earlier, the jazz musician of today is also inclined to compose new jazz tunes, and the new tunes are apt to contain similar melodic and harmonic formulas, similar forms, a steady pulse, and the other recognizable elements that place them in the American pop idiom. They are different but not radically so.

On the subject of jazz compositions (without lyrics), it is worthwhile to note a special practice that became prominent during the bop period (ca. 1940–1955). The players began to make up new melodies to fit older chord progressions, giving new titles to the finished products.

This practice works in the following manner: One takes the original chord progression formula from an older standard tune such as "I Got Rhythm," discards the original melody, composes a new melody that will be compatible with the "I Got Rhythm" chord progression, gives it a new title such as "Anthropology," and a new jazz composition is born. This became an established procedure, and a large body of new jazz tunes was produced in this way. Listed below are just a fraction of the many that were played and recorded:

45

NEW MELODY AND TITLE (called the "head")	ESTABLISHED CHORD FORMULA
"Anthropology"	"I Got Rhythm"
"Cheers"	"I Got Rhythm"
"52nd Street Theme"	"I Got Rhythm"
"Kim"	"I Got Rhythm"
"Merry Go-Round"	"I Got Rhythm"
"Oleo"	"I Got Rhythm"
"Shaw Nuff"	"I Got Rhythm"
"Bean at the Met"	"How High the Moon"
"Bird Lore"	"How High the Moon"
"Hopscotch"	"How High the Moon"
"Indiana Winter"	"How High the Moon"
"Low Ceiling"	"How High the Moon"
"Ornithology"	"How High the Moon"
"Slightly Dizzy"	"How High the Moon"
"Blue Serge"	"Cherokee"
"Dial-Ogue"	"Cherokee"
"Ko-Ko"	"Cherokee"
"Marshmallow"	"Cherokee"

A game played by musicians when hearing one of these tunes for the first time was to try to determine what the original tune was by listening to the chord progression. In order to make such a determination, one must have memorized the chord progressions of most of the existing standard tunes.

THE INSTRUMENTATION

Another important organizational factor in jazz is the *instrumentation* employed to present the basic tune. The music may be played by a fifty-piece studio orchestra, or it may be played by a trio of piano, bass, and drums or by any sized group in between these extremes. What follows is a list of instruments common in jazz performance. *Doubles* means that the instrumentalist is expected to be able to switch over to these other instruments and play them adequately.

BASIC	COMMON DOUBLES
Alto saxophone	Soprano saxophone, clarinet, flute, piccolo
Tenor saxophone	Same as above
Baritone saxophone	Clarinet, bass clarinet, flute, alto flute

Trumpet	Flugelhorn
Trombone	Bass trombone
Acoustic piano	Electronic keyboards
Electric bass	Arco bass
Electric guitar	Classical guitar
Drum set	Auxiliary percussion instruments

The preceding list contains the basic instruments used most of the time for jazz purposes. This does not mean, however, that other instruments cannot be used to play jazz. Jazz musicians have used harmonica, accordion, harpsichord, harp, oboe, bassoon, bagpipes, French horn, sitar, violin, cello, and many other instruments that might be considered to be outside the mainstream list just given.

It is not difficult to see that the basic instruments (wind instruments combined with chording instruments and drums) help to give jazz its distinctive character, clarity, and identity.

INSTRUMENTAL ROLES

The next consideration is how the instruments are used and how they are assigned different functional roles. In a large jazz ensemble the key players, the most crucially important players, are the drum set player and the lead trumpet player. The drummer keeps the steady pulse going, comments rhythmically on the other players' statements, fills in with small solos where there are open spots in the musical plan, and inserts rhythmic accents to highlight what the instrumental sections are declaring. But the pulse-keeping role remains the most important activity for the drummer.

The lead trumpet player sets the mode for phrasing, articulation, and overall style concept since the lead part is often the highest and most conspicuous. This player leads not only the trumpet section but the entire band in these respects and is the concert master of the large jazz ensemble, comparable to the first chair violinist in the symphony orchestra.

If either of these two players—the "pulse" player or the "melody" player—is lacking in skill and experience, the group will not sound sure and tight.

In a smaller combo, which may not utilize a trumpet, some other melodic instrument such as a woodwind or a guitar may assume the melody lead role. If the combo is smaller still, there may not be a drum set player, in which case the bass player may take on the pulse or time-keeping role. An accomplished jazz pianist alone can assume both the melodic lead role (with the right hand) and the pulse role (with the left hand).

An important organizational factor, then, is that these two roles, the pulse role and the melodic lead role, are assigned and heard.

FORMS

Another important organizational principle necessary to jazz performance is the total musical plan. This plan takes the form of a musical composition or arrangement. One hypothetical plan might be as follows:

> *Introduction* (sets the tempo, key, mood, and character)
> *Main Theme* (the central musical idea for the presentation)
> *Variations on the Theme* (in the form of solo improvisations)
> *Modulating Interlude* (moves the piece into another key)
> *Further Variations* (as written variations for the band)
> *Ending Section* (creates the effect of concluding the piece)

The preceding hypothetical plan is an outline of the *form* of the total piece. If it is an arrangement of an already existing tune, the orchestrator may take liberties with the original theme but still try to keep it recognizable. If it is a newly composed piece, the composer will use some sort of overall form similar to the above plan in order to give the piece breadth and dimension. Such plans are more necessary for large performing ensembles than they are for small combos. They are needed to keep the larger groups orderly and concerted.

A small combo may use fixed plans or arrangements in its normal repertoire, or the members may decide to play a piece they have never before performed. This performance may still sound quite polished and organized because the players are familiar with each other's procedures and techniques and can decide on the spur of the moment what shape the piece will take by using cues and signals within the group.

There is no one set plan for jazz arrangements and compositions, and the preceding plan is hypothetical only. A piece may take any one of a number of shapes. The essential ingredients, however, are the organized ensemble writing and playing and the opportunities for solo improvising.

The role of the arranger is quite important in ensemble performance, and the larger the ensemble the more crucial this role becomes. Exactly what is the arranger's function?

The scoring of an arrangement begins with the *lead sheet* for the tune being arranged for a jazz ensemble. This lead sheet contains the melody, the chord symbols, and perhaps the lyrics. The arranger then "arranges" this skeletal material into an orchestrated version so that each of the woodwinds, each brass player, and each member of the rhythm section has a separate written part. The arranger decides which key to place the piece in, what tempo should be used, and what pop or jazz style should be used. He or she decides on the form of the arrangement in choosing whether or not the piece will have an introduction, if there will be an extended ending, and if there is to be additional newly composed material. The arranger decides if the chords should be altered or if a countermelody should be added, and chooses throughout the arrangement which instruments to combine, how many to use, and which instruments to feature. Much of this work is actually composing, adding to the minimal lead sheet. (Many arrangers also compose original jazz pieces and songs.)

When scoring an orchestration, the arranger also decides if the saxophone players will double on flute or clarinet, if the trumpets or trombones will use mutes and, if so, which type of mute. He or she chooses the kinds of effects the electric guitar will use, the type of beat desired from the drummer, and the kind of *comping* needed from the pianist. The arranger also specifies the style of bass playing needed or writes a special part for the bassist. He or she chooses where the music will be soft and where it will be loud and, if the tempo changes, exactly where and how the effect will take place. And, most importantly, the arranger decides who will play jazz solos and where they will occur in the arrangement. All this information, and more, is placed in the conductor's score and in each instrumentalist's written part.

A successful jazz arrangement will contain a good jazz *paraphrase* of the original material, a valid swing feeling, and a certain amount of original jazz material composed by the arranger. The final product may be hack-work or it may be quite creative. Competent arrangers are always in demand for bands, shows, TV productions, and films. A few arrangers who have become well-known for their scoring skills are Fletcher Henderson, Duke Ellington, Quincy Jones,

Thad Jones, Gil Evans, Sammy Nestico, Neal Hefti, Sy Oliver, Pete Rugolo, and Toshiko Akiyoshi.

THE RHYTHMIC COMPLEX

The next organizational system to be investigated is the rhythmic complex. This organization of rhythms is present in most jazz efforts. The rhythmic complex is three-layered and simultaneous, and any one of the layers can be isolated and heard (see figure 6.11).

In a large jazz band, the important pulse instrument is the drums, and the drummer sets the time frame in which the piece will be performed. The bass player reinforces the time-keeping pulse, and there also may be a rhythm guitar to further reinforce the pulse. In addition, an auxiliary percussion instrument, such as conga drums, may contribute to the pulse. In a small combo, the drummer keeps the pulse and, if there is no drummer, the bassist will keep the pulse or a guitar may assume the pulse role. All of these possibilities come under background rhythm in figure 6.11. The role is essential for jazz performance but necessarily assumes a background position.

In the middleground lie *countermelody* and *chording*. Countermelody may be composed into an arrangement to complement a written melody or to complement an improvised solo. Countermelody may also be improvised by a melodic instrument in a combo. Although it is rhythmic and within the pulse of the piece, countermelody is not crucial to the overall rhythmic complex. Chording, however, does contribute to the middleground rhythm because it is more forceful

FIGURE 6.11.

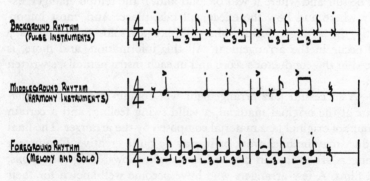

and because it is often presented in a syncopated rhythm which enhances the jazz or swing feeling of the piece. This effect is called *comping* and will be discussed at a later point. In the large jazz ensemble, the chording may be written into the score and performed by a group of instruments such as the sax section or the trombone section. It may also be performed by the pianist in an ad lib or free manner (the most common form of comping). In the smaller combo, the rhythmic chording may be performed by piano, guitar, or vibraphone. This layer of the rhythmic complex is more obvious and prominent than background and thus assumes a middleground role.

What is heard in the foreground of the rhythmic complex is what is most prominent—the melody, either in the form of a written theme or solo melodic improvisations. If the melody is the theme for a composition, it is recognized as such. If it is a paraphrased theme in an arrangement by an orchestrator, it is then recognized as a version, a variation, an interpretation of the original theme. If it appears in the form of solo improvisations on the theme, it is heard as a more remote variation of the theme. The soloist is then creating new melody to fit into the original form and to comply with the original chord progressions. Rhythmically, the foreground is often eighth notes, sixteenth notes, and other combinations of even faster rhythms.

These three rhythmic layers occur simultaneously in most jazz performances (see figure 6.12).

FIGURE 6.12.

Another important organizational factor to be considered in the presentation of jazz is the element of style. When a knowledgeable person speaks of jazz style, he or she is usually thinking of one of two things: a personal style of playing or a historical/geographical style.

In discussing a personal style, a saxophonist may be said to be playing in a style similar to Stan Getz or Johnny Hodges, or a drummer may be said to be playing in a style similar to Elvin Jones or Buddy Rich. What these musicians appear to be doing is utilizing some of the same musical mannerisms, some of the personal clichés, and, perhaps, in the case of wind instruments, using a tone quality, phrasing, and general instrumental sound similar to that of the original model.

A historical/geographical style is reflected in the stylistic differences between, for example, New Orleans Dixieland and Chicago Dixieland, or between white swing bands and black swing bands, or between bop and the cool jazz movement. These differences would include scoring, instrumentation, phrasing and articulation, solo differences, and rhythm section differences. Thus, one may recognize a style of jazz playing such as Chicago Dixieland because of the combination of instruments used, the scoring or plan for the ensemble playing, the manner in which the soloists improvise on the original composition, the manner in which the instruments phrase and articulate the music, and the manner of playing executed by the rhythm section.

Since jazz was invented at approximately the same time as was the phonograph, it is possible to study these historical/geographical styles in detail with recordings. The common historical/geographical styles are New Orleans Dixieland, Chicago Dixieland, Kansas City and black swing, white swing, bop, cool, hard bop, jazz-rock, and free jazz. In actual practice these styles are not always clear and distinct. Often, a well-known group will borrow elements from two or three different styles and will be an interesting-sounding band because they produce a kind of hybrid jazz sound.

SELF-RENEWAL

Lastly, the ongoing nature of jazz must be considered as an organizational concept. Because the one overriding principle is newness and renewal of melody (the solo improvisations), jazz must exist in a state of continuous change. It is not possible for jazz to advance without change and renewal. Through this process new forms evolve, new styles of playing and writing evolve, and, most importantly, new techniques and styles for improvising evolve. The only constant is change.

There is a duality in the competitiveness of jazz. First, the players and innovators are competitive among themselves, attempting to best each other and outdo each other. In the second sense, jazz is competitive in the marketplace. It must succeed commercially in order to survive. It is not heavily subsidized by grants, endowments, and bequests as are opera and the symphony orchestra. Still, jazz has endured for most of this century, and it continues to thrive and attract new generations of followers.

In review, the organizational elements of jazz are the music literature it uses (the American pop idiom), the instrumentation employed, the functional roles of the instruments, the plan or the arranger's score, the rhythmic complex, the stylistic characteristics, and the concept of change.

SUGGESTED RECORDS:

BOB MOVER, *Bob Mover*. Vanguard VSD-79408
JOHN COLTRANE, *The Best of John Coltrane*. Atlantic SD-1541
AL DIMEOLA, *Land of the Midnight Sun*. Columbia PC-34074
THAD JONES/MEL LEWIS, *The Jazz Orchestra*. Solid State SS-18003
LEE KONITZ, *The Lee Konitz Nonet*. Chiaroscuro CR-186
HORACE SILVER, *In Pursuit of the 27th Man*. Blue Note BN-LA054-F
SONNY STITT, *Constellation*. Cobblestone CST-9021
GARY BURTON/CHICK COREA, *Crystal Silence*. ECM 1024

SUGGESTIONS FOR LISTENING:

1. List the performances that are based on popular standard tunes.
2. List the performances that are based on newly composed jazz tunes.
3. In what ways is the music from the two groups similar?
4. From your listening, name the most basic or commonly used instruments.
5. Listen to a jazz arrangement and try to graph an outline of the form from beginning to end. (Name the sequence of events.)

6. Practice selective listening by trying to block out the foreground melody or solo and concetrating on (a) the middleground texture or (b) the background texture.

SUGGESTED FURTHER READINGS:

American Popular Song, Alec Wilder; Introduction, chapter 1.
Jazz Styles, Mark C. Gridley; Introduction, pp. 6 and 7, chapter 17.
Understanding Jazz, Leroy Ostransky; chapter 5.
Improvising Jazz, Jerry Coker; chapter 3.

CHAPTER SEVEN

IDENTIFYING JAZZ STYLES

SWING

Most (though not all) jazz efforts are said to swing. Yet, when one attempts to determine exactly what swing is, it becomes a bit elusive and difficult to define because swing is composed of several key ingredients, each of which contributes to the effect. Here are the necessary components:

1. The rhythmic complex, comprised of:
    (a) Steady pulse, unchanging tempo
    (b) Chording in syncopated rhythm
    (c) Melody with further syncopation
2. Interpretative freedom
3. Smooth ensemble power

These components can be explained as follows:

1. (a) The steady pulse within an unchanging tempo is maintained mostly by the rhythm section, primarily the drums and bass. The speed is constant, not slowing down or speeding up. This factor is traditional and came about because jazz bands played for dancing and dancers required a steady tempo. The players and orchestrators were compelled to get as much jazz excitement as possible from a restricted tempo frame. In addition to keeping the pulse, the rhythm section players overlaid it with syncopated rhythmic ideas to keep it animated.

1. (b) Further rhythmic interest is provided by chording in syncopated rhythms. (See Rhythmic Complex in chapter 6.) This syncopated chording (called comping) against the steady on-the-beat pulse seems to lift or bounce the music along. As was stated earlier, this effect may be achieved by a single keyboard player or guitarist, or by a group of instruments such as saxophones or trombones.

1. (c) Add to all this a further rhythmic interest in the form of a melody or a solo improvisation, either of which contains more syncopated rhythms. Expectancy, surprise, and excitement are now present.

2. A relaxed, loose interpretation is now added, a jazz feeling for playing the music, whether written out in notation or memorized. This would mean that it is not interpreted exactly but rather with a rhythmic looseness and freedom not present in the interpretation of so-called classical music.

3. When early jazz orchestrators such as Fletcher Henderson and Duke Ellington abandoned the Dixieland format of collective improvisation and took up scoring organized ensemble effects of a sax section, a trumpet section, a trombone section, and a rhythm section, the swing band was truly born because, in addition to the elements just listed, their bands acquired *smooth ensemble power*. This combination of sounds was irresistible to dancers. It also became an excellent texture against which to showcase jazz solos. It became known as "swing" and an entire historical period of music came to be called the "swing era."

Swing bands and the immensely popular dancing craze were made for each other. From the 1930s to the early 1950s, people danced to swing bands. There were no TV sets, no LP albums, no FM radios, and for an enjoyable evening a couple went to a movie or to a dance. In public ballrooms, nightclubs, gymnasiums, restaurants, hotels, roadhouses, living rooms, and Elk's Clubs, on ocean liners and front porches, or at street parties, people danced to swing bands.

Some idea of the rapport between a swinging band and the dancers, as well as some of the flavor of the music, can be obtained by reading the following excerpt from a review by Whitney Balliett for *The New Yorker:*

MONDAY: Al Cooper's Savoy Sultans, made up of two trumpets, three saxophones, and four rhythm, was the house band at the Savoy

Ballroom in Harlem from 1937 to 1945. It was a jump band—a rhythm machine that had one purpose: to make the customers dance their heads off. It did, and it generated such steam that it demolished all the alternating bands. (Earl Hines said, "The Sultans could swing you into bad health.") It was a primitive group, which played blues and the pop tunes of the day. The section work was offhand, the ensembles were riffs, the soloists were competent reproductions of Roy Eldridge and Coleman Hawkins. There were a lot of hustling black jump bands then (Sabby Lewis, Erskine Hawkins, the Mills Blue Rhythm Band), but none of their recordings capture what they sounded like in front of dancers. They were driving and free and exultant. They were showing off for the dancers, and the dancers, in return, showed off for them. It was a fervent, ritualistic relationship that made the music as close to visual as music can be. The drummer Panama Francis has resurrected the Sultans in the last year or so, and tonight he brought the band into Roseland. He had Franc Williams and Irving Stokes on trumpet, Bill Easley and Howard Johnson on alto saxophones, George Kelly, who was a member of the original Sultans, on tenor saxophone, Red Richards on piano, John Smith on guitar, and Bill Pemberton on bass. They played two sets of standards, riff blues, ballads, and old Sultan arrangements, and caused consternation and delight. Francis, a somewhat heavy Chick Webb drummer overlaid with Sid Catlett traceries, played like a madman. He pushed and roared, and one could almost see the music catapulting off the bandstand, lifting the meanest dancer, exalting the best.[1]

Swing bands were broadcast live on AM radio from famous ballrooms all across the United States and could be heard late at night on any home or car radio. There was a thriving swing band record industry (78 rpm), enabling one to have a dance party at home with the aid of a record player.

It was inevitable that these bands would become known as dance bands, and since form often follows function, some band leaders concentrated on danceable, commercial orchestrations wherein the melody was always readily recognizable, the swing sound was minimal, and the jazz solos were practically nonexistent. Some of these bands were quite successful and continued for years to follow the same patterns. They earned wide public recognition, sold many records, and were in demand for engagements as often as they wished, but they were not swing bands; they were commercial dance bands.

The reader may well be confused by the swing band/dance band labeling, and this is quite understandable. Confusion may exist because some of the well-known swing bands, famous for their dance music, did not emphasize jazz to any great degree (Tommy Dorsey, Glenn Miller). Conversely, others did emphasize jazz while functioning for dance purposes (Count Basie, Woody Herman). And still others did nothing with jazz and concentrated only on playing danceable music (Guy Lombardo). The fact that some of these bands are still working today adds to the confusion. Basie and Herman seldom play for dancing any more, most of the time playing only jazz concerts. "Ghost bands" are operating today (The Glenn Miller Orchestra, conducted by _____, the Tommy Dorsey Orchestra, conducted by _____). And Lawrence Welk will occasionally feature a jazz soloist (but only for TV show-biz purposes). Some successful bands from the swing era may be categorized into three groups: (1) swing bands that featured jazz arrangements and jazz soloists, (2) swing bands that functioned as dance bands but featured some jazz, and (3) dance bands that featured little or no jazz.

Here is a partial list of bands that were essentially swing bands. Although they played for dancing, they featured jazz soloists and jazz arrangements:

The Count Basie Orchestra	The Charlie Barnet Orchestra
The Duke Ellington Orchestra	The Les Brown Orchestra
The Jimmie Lunceford Orchestra	The Woody Herman Orchestra
	The Artie Shaw Orchestra
The Roy Eldridge Orchestra	The Benny Goodman Orchestra
The Benny Carter Orchestra	The Harry James Orchestra
The Earl Hines Orchestra	The Buddy Rich Orchestra
The Lionel Hampton Orchestra	The Bunny Berigan Orchestra
The Chick Webb Orchestra	The Gene Krupa Orchestra
The Benny Moten Orchestra	The Bob Crosby Orchestra
The Erskine Hawkins Orchestra	The Stan Kenton Orchestra

Some of the leaders just mentioned are still active musicians but no longer front a band regularly. Others, such as Count Basie and Woody Herman, have become jazz patriarchs. They kept their bands together through good times and bad, and now, with the renewed interest in jazz, they are more popular than ever.

Here is a partial list of swing bands that were used primarily for dancing but which featured some jazz:

The Vaughn Monroe Orchestra	The Ralph Flanagan Orchestra
The Ray Anthony Orchestra	The Sam Donahue Orchestra
The Tony Pastor Orchestra	The Jerry Wald Orchestra
The Claude Thornhill Orchestra	The Ted Heath Orchestra

The Glenn Miller Orchestra
The Tommy Dorsey Orchestra
The Jimmy Dorsey Orchestra
The Sonny Dunham Orchestra
The Billy Butterfield Orchestra
The Billy May Orchestra
The Lee Castle Orchestra

The Will Bradley/Ray McKinley Orchestra
The Hal McIntyre Orchestra
The Charlie Spivak Orchestra
The Les Elgart Orchestra
The Ralph Marterie Orchestra

This in-between group is the most difficult of the three to label. The following is a partial list of dance bands that were well-known in the swing era. Their function was to provide dance music, and they featured little or no jazz:

The Sammy Kaye Orchestra
The Chuck Foster Orchestra
The Clyde McCoy Orchestra
The Jan Garber Orchestra
The Shep Fields Orchestra
The Blue Barron Orchestra
The Larry Clinton Orchestra
The Guy Lombardo Orchestra
The Russ Morgan Orchestra
The Art Mooney Orchestra
The Tommy Tucker Orchestra
The Frankie Carle Orchestra
The Kay Kyser Orchestra
The Eddie Howard Orchestra

The Carmen Cavallaro Orchestra
The Henry Busse Orchestra
The Dick Jurgens Orchestra
The Ozzie Nelson Orchestra
The Hal Kemp Orchestra
The Glen Gray Orchestra
The Ray Noble Orchestra
The Freddie Martin Orchestra
The Johnny Long Orchestra
The Alvino Rey Orchestra
The Bob Astor Orchestra
The Lawrence Welk Orchestra
The Jan Savitt Orchestra

Many of these bands had national reputations as a result of weekly radio shows and recordings. Others, such as Blue Barron, Johnny Long, and Lawrence Welk, were regional bands but had substantial reputations, often the result of a popular recording.

Lastly, the dozens of little-known territory bands should be mentioned. These were bands that traveled in a geographic area, often many miles from their home towns, in order to play dances. They were made up of musicians who may have held day jobs and who played several nights a week on the road. Some of these bands played special arrangements, employed fine players, and were interesting to hear. Others used stock arrangements purchased at the local music store, employed mediocre players, and made unimaginative music. Territory bands were, however, a training ground for many future jazz stars.

The word "swing" still is used to describe a driving jazz performance. A "swinger" is a cool, perceptive person. A jazz group "swings," a player "swings," an orchestration "swings."

PERSONAL STYLES

There are schools of saxophone playing, trumpet playing, trombone playing, piano playing, drumming; that is, there are particular styles of playing. Why will one saxophonist sound a great deal like some other saxophonist? Why does one drummer sound like another drummer? Why does Miles Davis sound different from most trumpet players? Why does Johnny Griffin sound different from most tenor saxophonists? The components of a personal instrumental style can be recognized by the listener. The presence of certain of these components, plus the player's experience and inner concept of melody making, gives the player a distinctive style. That style can be described using the following characteristics.

WIND INSTRUMENT PLAYER'S STYLISTIC COMPONENTS

1. *Tone quality:* rough and raspy or smooth and clear; bright or dark; soft, medium, or loud; vibrato or no vibrato; mutes.
2. *Ranges used:* favors low register, middle, high, or extremely high register (altissimo) of the instrument.
3. *Phrasing:* short, choppy phrases or long, rambling phrases; a mixing of phrase lengths; continuous playing or use of rests for phrase punctuation.
4. *Melodic treatment:* original melody with ornaments; paraphrase of original melody; little or no reference to original melody.
5. *Improvising technique:* chord arpeggiation; scales; patterns; sequence; clichés; quotes; unusual personal patterns; number of notes per beat; repetition; vocal effects; eccentric mannerisms.

PIANIST'S STYLISTIC COMPONENTS

1. *Textures:* favors single-note melody for right hand, octaves for right hand; walking bass for left hand, chords for left hand; stride; melodic coupling; two-hand octaves; counterpoint; chordal densities; tremolo.

60

2. *Ranges used:* favors low, middle, or high section of keyboard.
3. *Comping:* sketchy, open accompanying for soloist or tight, dense accompaniment; pulse-keeping accompaniment or free and syncopated.
4. *Phrasing:* short, choppy phrases or long, rambling phrases; a mixing of phrase lengths; continuous playing or use of rests for phrase punctuation.
5. *Melodic treatment:* original melody with ornaments; paraphrase of original melody; little or no reference to original melody.
6. *Improvising technique:* chord arpeggiation; scales; patterns; sequence; clichés; quotes; unusual personal patterns; number of notes per beat; repetition; eccentric mannerisms.

GUITARIST'S STYLISTIC COMPONENTS

1. *Tone quality:* acoustic or electric body; pick or finger; amplifiers and electronic equipment such as tone control, tremolo, reverb, fuzz, wah-wah, tone dividers, phase shifter, tape echo.
2. *Textures:* single-note melody; double stops; arpeggios; octaves; slide bar; tremolo; glisses; bending notes; string vibrato; finger vibrato; chordal densities.
3. *Ranges used:* favors low, middle, or high register of the instrument.
4. *Comping:* sketchy, open accompanying for soloist or tight, dense accompaniment; pulse-keeping rhythm guitar or free and syncopated.
5. *Phrasing:* short, choppy phrases or long, rambling phrases; a mixing of phrase lengths; continuous playing or use of rests for phrase punctuation.
6. *Melodic treatment:* original melody with ornaments; paraphrase of original melody; little or no reference to original melody.
7. *Improvising techniques:* chord arpeggiation; scales; patterns; sequence; clichés; quotes; unusual personal patterns; number of notes per beat; repetition; eccentric mannerisms.

BASSIST'S STYLISTIC COMPONENTS

1. *Tone quality:* electric or acoustic (upright); plucked or bowed (pizzicato or arco); amplifiers and electronic equipment as for guitar.
2. *Textures:* single-note melody; double stops; strumming all four strings; glisses; bending notes; vibrato.
3. *Ranges used:* favors low, middle, or high register of instrument.
4. *Comping:* walking bass; double-time comping; conversational response to others in group.

5. *Phrasing:* short phrases; long phrases; a mixing of phrase lengths; continuous playing or use of random silences.
6. *Melodic treatment:* original melody with ornaments; melodic paraphrase; little or no reference to original melody.
7. *Improvising techniques:* chord arpeggiation; scales; patterns; sequence; clichés; quotes; unusual personal patterns; number of notes per beat; repetition; eccentric mannerisms.

DRUMMER'S STYLISTIC COMPONENTS

1. *Tone quality:* choice of color of cymbals—bright or dark, and color of drums—dry (tight tuning) or wet (loose tuning); personal use of brushes, sticks, and mallets; soft, medium, or loud playing; dampening of drums or cymbals.
2. *Textures:* favors cymbal textures, drum textures, or a consistent mix; favors certain cymbals (ride, crash, or hi-hat cymbal) or favors certain drums (snare, tom-tom, or bass drum); favors an open, skeletal texture or a busy, multilevel texture with several simultaneous beat patterns.
3. *Time keeping:* keeps ride rhythm on the ride cymbal, on the hi-hat cymbal, or on the snare drum; accents and fills on the snare drum, the bass drum, or the crash cymbal; time keeping exactly on the beat or pushing slightly on top of each beat; use of *feed-ins* to ensemble phrases; personal *fill* style; sensitivity to the group's playing and to the style of the piece being played.
4. *Improvising or solo style:* solos in time or abandons time keeping for solo; ability to return to the original tempo; solos consisting of drum rudiments or colors, contrasts, and blends; continuous solos or sectioned with breaks dividing sections; ability to create dramatic subtleties and climaxes.

By using the preceding component guides, one may begin to understand why one player sounds something like another, or why one player is unlike others and therefore is recognizable by his sound alone. These guides will also make it easier to compare two players who play the same instrument.

SAMPLE SOLO ANALYSIS

It would now be beneficial to apply the stylistic component guides to an actual solo in order to make some detailed observations. (References will also be made to figures 9.1 through 9.8 in chapter 9.)

The soloist chosen is Charlie Parker and the recorded solo cho-

sen is his alto sax solo on "Ko Ko." This was originally recorded on a
78-rpm, 10-inch disc in 1945. The label was Savoy 597-B, and the ensemble listed on the label included Charlie Parker, alto sax; Miles
Davis, trumpet; Hen Gates, piano; Curley Russell, bass; and Max
Roach, drums. The label is, however, apparently erroneous. The
trumpet player is almost surely not Miles but Dizzy Gillespie, and the
pianist "Hen Gates" is also probably Dizzy, using a pseudonym. This
recording is available in the *Smithsonian Collection of Classic Jazz* and is
therefore not obscure or difficult to obtain.

"KO KO"

Alto Sax solo by Charlie Parker

• Original tune: "Cherokee" by Ray Noble.

• Form: 32-bar pop standard, AABA (see chapter 6). Parker
uses 8-bar phrases instead of 4-bar phrases, and thus each section is 16
measures in length instead of 8 measures.

• Tempo: medium-fast.

• Total number of choruses (times) played by soloist: two.
(There is not much room on a 10-inch 78 to "stretch out.")

• Placement of solo in the arrangement: intro consisting of a
trumpet-alto unison melody followed by very brief individual horn
solos and another short unison statement. Parker's two-chorus solo
follows. After the alto solo there is a rather extended drum solo followed by a composed ending using thematic material from the intro.

The following observations may be made, referring to the wind instrument stylistic components guide:

1. *Tone quality:* clear, bright, medium-loud, no vibrato. (Parker was the
   model for bop-period alto sax tone.)
2. *Ranges used:* Parker favors his middle register most of the time. He
   uses a low register tone only occasionally and does not use the extreme high register at all.
3. *Phrasing:* Parker mixes phrase lengths. Some are as short as 1 measure
   (4 or 5 beats) and at least two are as long as 7 measures (28 beats).
   There is much variety in phrase lengths, and rests are used in between for punctuation.

4. *Melodic treatment:* There is no reference to the original "Cherokee" melody. The solo is a total improvisation from beginning to end.

5. *Improvising techniques:* (Also see figures 9.1-9.8 in chapter 9.) Parker does use *chord arpeggiation,* both ascending and descending. He combines these with *scales* and *scale fragments.* In this solo a favorite *personal pattern* appears several times. This consists of an ascending chord arpeggiation connected to a descending scale fragment. He uses *sequence* several times (also a favorite device), and he shifts it around rhythmically to keep it interesting. He does not often *quote* in his solos and this one is no exception. Parker does use a *personal rhythmic pattern* several times in this solo. It is a Parker "thumbprint" and is most often used to conclude a phrase. It consists of several eighth notes followed immediately by a longer tone. It should be noted that in the bop period jazz soloing more often occurred in consecutive eighth notes than in any other note lengths. The *number of notes per beat* in this solo is mainly two eighth notes per beat, but Parker does on several occasions use triplet groups of eighths (three eighths per beat) and this figure is often used to begin a phrase. In the bridge of the second chorus (the B section), Parker uses a descending sequence built of groups of six sixteenth notes plus one final eighth. *Repetition* is also a part of Parker's improvising technique, but a phrase is seldom repeated exactly. Some slight modification is usually incorporated into the repeated material. For example, the second phrase of the solo, a short phrase, is immediately repeated, but careful listening reveals that the first note has been lowered one-half tone. A different use of *repetition* is heard when the first phrase of the solo, a 4-measure phrase, is compared to the phrase that begins the second A section. The phrase is altered at its start but then becomes identical to the first phrase for the balance of its length.

Certain melodic and rhythmic gestures used by the soloist, as well as his tone quality, help us to recognize him. His techniques help to identify him. The creative uses of technique, the seemingly endless connecting processes involved in its use, makes a virtuoso improviser fascinating to hear. For purposes of analysis, individual elements of the solo have been noted, but it is the creative process of combining them in different and original ways that makes the solo meaningful and attractive.

The foregoing wind instrument guide was useful in making detailed observations regarding the Parker sax solo. One may also make similar observations for a piano solo, a guitar solo, a bass solo, or a drum solo using the guides for those instruments.

The alto solo was a short one. If an extended solo of several choruses is analyzed, one may be able to graph different degrees of intensity and energy and also locate climactic points.

ADVANCED IMPROVISATION

The personal styles of many skilled players include advanced improvisational techniques. In the past, many professionals had long and successful careers with only modest improvising abilities, but new music and new styles in playing have made it imperative for a competitive jazz player to keep up with the more technically difficult improvising skills. Today's gifted virtuoso improvisers may utilize the following:

- *Odd meters:* The ability to improvise in metric schemes other than $\frac{2}{4}$, $\frac{4}{4}$, or $\frac{3}{4}$. Dave Brubeck and Don Ellis pioneered improvisation in nonsymmetrical meters such as $\frac{5}{4}$, $\frac{5}{8}$, $\frac{7}{4}$, $\frac{7}{8}$, $\frac{11}{8}$, etc. Some advanced improvisers can create interesting solos in these meters as easily as in $\frac{4}{4}$.

- *Keys:* Early jazz players usually played in a limited number of keys. Today, the skilled improviser can play a creative solo in any key and possesses the ability to modulate from one key to another as part of the presentation.

- *Tempos:* The gifted improviser has the ability to improvise at extremely fast tempos while remaining controlled and lucid.

- *Playing in time:* A difficult variant of this necessary ability is to be able to maintain time in an unaccompanied solo without the presence of a drummer or any sort of rhythm section assistance. The soloist must play in such a way as to keep the listener informed at all times about where he or she is in the original tune. This is a difficult feat to bring off successfully and requires practice and experience. One is, in effect, playing a melodic instrument while at the same time implying harmony (a comping function) and time (a rhythm section function).

- *Limited structure:* The advanced improviser has the ability to create a solo while the harmonic support is limited to only one or two chords, a drone harmonic interval, or a repeated bass figure. At first glance this may seem relatively easy, since the player does not have to follow a structured chord progression format. It is precisely because of the dearth of chord changes that such a situation is often difficult for the improviser. In the absence of a structured piece of music to build upon, the improviser's problem is to construct an interesting solo with a beginning, a middle, and an end. This is a formidable task for the conscientious improviser.

• *Free jazz:* Some free jazz operates within a musical plan that has no pulse (time), tone center (key), or theme on which to build a solo. Usually, though, at least one of these factors is present. If the presentation is without a time frame, the drummer often presents the impression of pulse keeping, playing in such a way as to maintain an energy level. This can create the impression of a fast tempo (high energy level) or a slow tempo (low energy level). The soloist proceeds within the same energy level in his or her conception of the solo. If there is no recognizable key, there may still be a recurring return to a particular pitch, which, by repetition, emphasizes this note and creates the impression that this note is the tonal center of the presentation. If there is no such emphasis in the comping, the soloist may insert such emphasis in the solo. If there is no recognizable theme, the soloist may invent a motive, a short theme of two or three notes, and construct a solo from it. Obviously, all of these concepts in this type of free jazz demand a cerebral soloing and a superb instrumental facility. The novice simply doesn't have the experience for this. Nor can it be fully enjoyed by the novice listener for precisely the same reason.

SPECIALIZED INSTRUMENTAL TECHNIQUES

Finally, there are specialized instrumental techniques that become part of the advanced improviser's personal style. Several of these advanced techniques involve playing an instrument in an unconventional manner. If this is done just as a gimmick, the gimmickry is usually obvious. If, on the other hand, the technique is adopted in an artistic way to enhance the solo, the effect can be breathtaking. Here are several frequently used examples:

1. Simultaneously singing while blowing a flute.
2. Simultaneously singing while bowing a string bass.
3. Singing through a saxophone.
4. Using the altissimo register of a saxophone. (By learning special fingerings, a saxophonist may play extremely high notes on the instrument.)
5. Extreme glissando on woodwind and brass instruments. (*Glissando* means to slide smoothly from one pitch to another so that the separate pitches are not discernible.)
6. Circular breathing for wind instruments. (Circular breathing describes a way of blowing wherein the player seemingly never pauses to take a breath; this is accomplished by quickly storing air in the

cheeks and, while expelling this air, quickly taking more air in through the nostrils.)

7. Performing on the strings of a piano.
8. Performing in quarter-tones. (Some Oriental tonal systems use scale steps that are smaller than the western tempered scale system. To find them on a western keyboard, extra keys would be needed in between the present keys. Wind and string instrumentalists can approximate these pitches.)
9. Performing with Echoplex or other electronic devices. (An artistic concept is required for artisitic results.)

HISTORICAL STYLES

In addition to discussing the swing style and a player's personal style, a jazz style may also be related to jazz history. It is not the author's intent to rework jazz history; this has been discussed in detail in several excellent books on the subject. What is presented here is merely a broad outline that will show the scope of the subject and the material. *Note:* The following descriptions are generalizations based on a norm and do not include an occasional variant or exception.

NEW ORLEANS DIXIELAND (ca. 1900–1920)

• *Instrumentation:* Cornet, clarinet, trombone, piano, drums, banjo (not always), bass (not always).

• *Ensemble characteristics:* Collective improvisational texture prevailed; cornet played the melody with ornaments and elaborations; clarinet complemented cornet with a harmony part above the melody, often in the form of a florid *obbligato;* trombone played simple, bass-like figures.

• *Solo characteristics:* Solos were infrequent and took the form of modified melody with elaborations; phrasing was ordinarily in 2- or 4-bar phrases.

• *Rhythm section characteristics:* Straight 4 beats per measure without accents, mostly simple time keeping; chording instruments used same rhythm.

• *Notable bands:* King Oliver and his Creole Jazz Band, Original Dixieland Jazz Band.

- *Performers:*

Cornet	*Clarinet*
Buddy Bolden	Johnny Dodds
Joe "King" Oliver	Barney Bigard
Louis Armstrong	Omer Simeon
Bunk Johnson	Jimmy Noone
Nick LaRocca	*Drums*
Freddie Keppard	Baby Dodds
Mutt Carey	Tony Sbarbaro
Trombone	*Piano*
Honore Dutrey	Lil Hardin Armstrong
Kid Ory	Jelly Roll Morton
Soprano Sax	Fate Marable
Sidney Bechet	

It is difficult to know positively how New Orleans Dixieland sounded because of the scarcity of recordings from this early period and because of the poor quality of the reproductions.

CHICAGO DIXIELAND (ca. 1925–1930)

This style was the model for all future Dixieland playing.

- *Instrumentation:* Cornet or trumpet, clarinet, saxophone, trombone, piano, bass, drums, guitar (not always).

- *Ensemble characteristics:* Less relaxed, more ensemble drive, more attention paid to form with elaborate ensemble intros, interludes, and endings; also more emphasis on solos as an important part of the presentation; cornet or trumpet were still dominant as lead instruments with other wind instruments as harmony or countermelody; ensemble improvisation was still important to this music.

- *Solo characteristics:* Ornamented original melody or arpeggiated chord melody; use of mutes, glissando, and shakes; 2- or 4-bar phrasing still prevailed.

- *Rhythm section characteristics:* Straight 4 beats per measure with accents on 2 and 4; chording instruments strummed without accents; some drum solos or breaks; more attention to tuning drum set.

- *Notable bands:* New Orleans Rhythm Kings, Louis Armstrong's Hot Five and Hot Seven, the Wolverines.

- *Performers:*

Cornet
Bix Beiderbecke
Muggsy Spanier
Trumpet
Jimmy McPartland
Wingy Manone
Bunny Berigan
Trombone
Miff Mole
Jack Teagarden
J. C. Higginbotham
Saxophone
Frankie Trumbauer
Frank Teschemacher
Bud Freeman

Clarinet
Pee Wee Russell
Mezz Mezzrow
Jimmy Dorsey
Guitar
Eddie Condon
Piano
Joe Sullivan
Drums
Dave Tough
Gene Krupa
George Wettling

At this time, transplanted New Orleans musicians were working in Chicago and developing jazz in different styles.

KANSAS CITY AND BLACK SWING (ca. 1925–1950)

- *Instrumentation:* Three to five saxes, two to five trumpets, one to four trombones, piano, bass, drums, guitar (not always).

- *Ensemble characteristics:* Played standards, ballads, and riff blues; section writing replaced Dixieland collective improvisation, and arrangers and composers became important; articulated but smooth phrasing with legato tonguing; call and response between sections, block chord voicing, or unison writing for ensemble; swing eighth-note scoring prevailed, and all performed in a loose, relaxed manner.

- *Solo characteristics:* Repeated notes and repeated patterns in solos reflected style of riff arrangements; also used arpeggiated chord melody and scalar melody; used mutes, scooping, and vocal effects on instruments; solos utilized no vibrato or a very wide, dramatic vibrato; generally 2- or 4-bar phrasing.

- *Rhythm section characteristics:* Drummer used hi-hat cymbal for keeping time, ride cymbal for additional power and time, crash cymbal and bass drum for accenting the ensemble; drummer played fills and commented rhythmically on ensemble and solo statements; accents on 2 and 4, or shuffle rhythm was common; walking bass with emphasis on strong chord tones; piano comped rhythmically and played fills; guitar seldom soloed and played unobtrusive time.

• *Notable bands:* The Fletcher Henderson Orchestra, the Count Basie Orchestra, the Duke Ellington Orchestra, the Jimmie Lunceford Orchestra, the Chick Webb Orchestra, the Andy Kirk Orchestra, the Cab Calloway Orchestra.

• *Performers:*

Trumpet	*Alto Sax*
Roy Eldridge	Marshall Royal
Charlie Shavers	Johnny Hodges
Hot Lips Page	Benny Carter
Cat Anderson	Russell Procope
Cootie Williams	*Baritone Sax*
Rex Stewart	Harry Carney
Clark Terry	*Piano*
Harry "Sweets" Edison	Art Tatum
Thad Jones	Count Basie
Snooky Young	Duke Ellington
Tenor Sax	Teddy Wilson
Coleman Hawkins	Nat Cole
Lester Young	Erroll Garner
Ben Webster	Milt Buckner
Chu Berry	*Clarinet*
Don Byas	Barney Bigard
Paul Gonsalves	Buster Bailey
Herschel Evans	Jimmy Hamilton
Buddy Tate	Russell Procope
Wardell Gray	*Drums*
Lucky Thompson	Jo Jones
Illinois Jacquet	Sid Catlett
Eddie "Lockjaw" Davis	Chick Webb
Frank Foster	Sonny Greer
Frank Wess	Cozy Cole
Trombone	*Bass*
Dickie Wells	Jimmy Blanton
Lawrence Brown	John Kirby
Joe "Tricky Sam" Nanton	Oscar Pettiford
Tyree Glenn	*Guitar*
Trummy Young	Charlie Christian

Note: Alto, tenor, and baritone saxophone became standard. The C melody, bass, and soprano saxes became obsolete. (The soprano would become popular again in the 1960s.)

WHITE SWING (ca. 1935–1950)

- *Instrumentation:* Three to five saxes, two to five trumpets, one to four trombones, piano, bass, drums, guitar (not always).

- *Ensemble characteristics:* Played standards, ballads, and specials based on riff blues; adopted black swing style of sectional scoring; hard tonguing prevailed and phrasing used more slurring than black swing; emphasized tight, "as one" ensemble playing with stress on precision and blend; fast vibrato; notation was read as accurately as possible.

- *Solo characteristics:* Ornamented melody, paraphrase, or arpeggiated chord melody; fast vibrato was common; 2-or 4-bar phrasing prevailed.

- *Rhythm section characteristics:* Drummer kept time with bass drum, played straight 4 beats per measure with accents on 2 and 4, and often played ride time on hi-hat foot cymbal as well; drummer played fewer fills than black drummers and was less adventurous on solos; bass outlined strong chord tones in walking style; piano played mostly stride or straight 4 comping; guitar played straight 4 chording rhythm.

- *Notable bands:* The Benny Goodman Orchestra, the Artie Shaw Orchestra, the Woody Herman Orchestra, the Charlie Barnet Orchestra, the Glenn Miller Orchestra, the Tommy Dorsey Orchestra, the Jimmy Dorsey Orchestra, the Claude Thornhill Orchestra, the Les Brown Orchestra, the Harry James Orchestra, the Stan Kenton Orchestra.

- *Performers:*

Trumpet	*Piano*
Conte Candoli	Jess Stacy
Ray Wetzel	Mel Powell
Sonny Berman	Joe Bushkin
Bunny Berigan	*Trombone*
Harry James	Tommy Dorsey
Bobby Hackett	Bill Harris
Tenor Sax	Frank Rosolino
Charlie Barnet	*Alto Sax*
Bob Cooper	Jimmy Dorsey
Georgie Auld	Johnny Bothwell
Vido Musso	Art Pepper
Flip Phillips	Woody Herman

Bass	Drums
Eddie Safranski	Gene Krupa
Arnold Fishkin	Louis Bellson
Chubby Jackson	Buddy Rich
Clarinet	Dave Tough
Benny Goodman	*Guitar*
Artie Shaw	Barney Kessel
Woody Herman	Herb Ellis
Jimmy Dorsey	
Buddy DeFranco	

BOP (ca. 1940–1955)

• *Instrumentation:* Usually a combo, the quintet being more or less typical and consisting of one sax (alto or tenor), one trumpet (or trombone), piano, bass, and drums; vibraphone was popular, guitar was often used, and flute began to become popular; clarinet became quite rare.

• *Ensemble characteristics:* Dance tempos were no longer a consideration, so tempos (especially for combo) were often quite fast; ensemble effect was predicated on the *head* (theme) being played by melodic instruments in unison, backed by syncopated comping and rhythm playing; standards or new bop tunes were in vogue; no vibrato.

• *Solo characteristics:* Solo performance was stressed over the ensemble; multiple choruses became common (long, extended solos) and speed and technique became advanced; phrase lengths were not symmetrical or predictable; solos in sixteenth and thirty-second notes became common; usually no vibrato; solos were made up of scales, arpeggiated chords, and sequence.

• *Rhythm section characteristics:* More continuous sound from the drummer but also more sensitivity; drummer used hi-hat foot cymbal on 2 and 4 and a sustained ringing on ride cymbal; lots of accents and fills on snare drum, only accents on bass drum; piano comped in syncopation, filled, and sometimes commented with countermelody; bass used walking patterns, which became more elaborate and melodic; guitar became more pianistic in comping role—not just simple strumming.

• *Notable bands:* Although bop was more often a combo music, a few big bands that tried to incorporate bop style were the Woody

Herman Orchestra, the Claude Thornhill Orchestra, the Stan Kenton Orchestra, the Dizzy Gillespie Big Band.

- *Performers:*

Trumpet	Baritone Sax
Dizzy Gillespie	Cecil Payne
Fats Navarro	Serge Chaloff
Clifford Brown	*Bass*
Howard McGhee	Oscar Pettiford
Miles Davis	Ray Brown
Clark Terry	Percy Heath
Tenor Sax	*Guitar*
Dexter Gordon	Kenny Burrell
Sonny Rollins	Tal Farlow
Zoot Sims	*Alto Sax*
Stan Getz	Charlie Parker
Johnny Griffin	Sonny Stitt
Allen Eager	James Moody
Charlie Ventura	Boots Mussulli
Don Byas	Phil Woods
Gene Ammons	*Drums*
Piano	Kenny Clarke
Thelonious Monk	Max Roach
Bud Powell	Roy Haynes
George Shearing	Denzil Best
Oscar Peterson	*Vibes*
Trombone	Milt Jackson
J. J. Johnson	Terry Gibbs
Kai Winding	
Jimmy Cleveland	

COOL AND WEST COAST (ca. 1949–1955)

- *Instrumentation:* As with bop, the combo was the important ensemble, a typical one consisting of two horns, perhaps a guitar, piano, bass, and drums.

- *Ensemble characteristics:* Subdued, light, subtle sound with no vibrato, hence the label "cool"; controlled unison horn playing often in very fast tempos; original scoring showed an outgrowth of bop melody, sometimes with intricate rhythms, surprising phrasings, and silences.

- *Solo characteristics:* Less heat than bop solos; breathy horn sound without vibrato; a "pretty" or classical kind of playing prevailed, and smooth, thoughtful soloing became important.

- *Rhythm section characteristics:* Similar to bop but a much quieter approach; drummers paid more attention to tuning the drum set and began to play melodically using cymbal colors, brushes, and soft mallets in addition to the usual time-keeping techniques; piano used more smooth-moving block chords, less rhythmic punch; bass played time using walking patterns; guitar played melodic figures.

- *Notable bands:* The Claude Thornhill Orchestra, the Dave Brubeck Quartet, the Miles Davis Nonet, the Gerry Mulligan Quartet.

- *Performers:*

Trumpet
Miles Davis
Chet Baker
Shorty Rogers
Conte Candoli
Tenor Sax
Zoot Sims
Wayne Marsh
Buddy Collette
Richie Kamuca
Dave Pell
Jimmy Giuffre (all saxes, clarinets and flute)
Trombone
Bob Brookmeyer
Frank Rosolino
Baritone Sax
Gerry Mulligan
Piano
Lennie Tristano
Dave Brubeck
Hampton Hawes

Vibes
Teddy Charles
Alto Sax
Lee Konitz
Paul Desmond
Art Pepper
Bud Shank
Drums
Chico Hamilton
Shelley Manne
Stan Levey
Bass
Red Mitchell
Red Callender
Guitar
Howard Roberts
Barney Kessel

HARD BOP (ca. 1955–1965)

- *Instrumentation:* Combo or expanded combo with saxes, brass, piano, bass, and drums; sometimes organ replaced piano, and guitar was sometimes used; soprano sax became popular.

- *Ensemble characteristics:* A return to heated playing and ensemble sounds; gospel chord progressions, harmonies, and soul replaced cool concepts; funky, blues-like thematic ideas became popular; a development of forms and phrase lengths in composed pieces.

- *Solo characteristics:* Earthy, brassy tone quality for saxes and trumpet; expansion of bop improvisation techniques—short, explosive ideas interspersed with long, technically dazzling phrases, sometimes with a wide, deliberate vibrato.

- *Rhythm section characteristics:* A driving, busy drum style which placed drums in the foreground on a more equal status with soloists, interacting with them; piano style often used repeated melodic figures instead of chord comping; bass players used horn soloists as models for melodic lines, giving bass lines thrust and drive.

- *Notable bands:* Cannonball Adderly groups, Freddie Hubbard groups, Art Blakey groups.

- *Performers:*

Trumpet
Freddie Hubbard
Lee Morgan
Donald Byrd
Blue Mitchell
Kenny Dorham
Trombone
J. J. Johnson
Jimmy Knepper
Jimmy Cleveland
Bass
Paul Chambers
Wilbur Ware
Percy Heath
Alto Sax
Cannonball Adderly
Jackie McLean
Phil Woods
Gigi Gryce
Tenor Sax
Sonny Rollins
John Coltrane
Frank Foster
Stanley Turrentine
Joe Henderson
Wayne Shorter
Hank Mobley

Baritone Sax
Cecil Payne
Pepper Adams
Guitar
Wes Montgomery
Kenny Burrell
Drums
Philly Jo Jones
Roy Haynes
Elvin Jones
Max Roach
Art Blakey
Mickey Roker
Jimmy Cobb
Piano
Horace Silver
Ramsey Lewis
Tommy Flanagan
Joe Zawinul
Organ
Jimmy Smith
Don Patterson
Larry Young

JAZZ ROCK (CURRENT)

- *Instrumentation:* May be a big band with electronic rhythm section (electronic keyboards, electric bass, electric guitar, drums, and additional percussionists) or a rock combo with assorted horns; sophisticated electronic gear often used on the horns to distort the tone quality.

- *Ensemble characteristics:* Contains the high energy and tension of rock bands with repeated bass figures, simple rock harmonies, funky melodic ideas, and some use of modal materials; much activity from the drummer, and extra percussionists used for Latin American and African percussion instruments; drum set tuned for a loose, soggy sound; some scores contain a stable, floating tune against an active rhythm section; some scoring is serene and pastoral; collective improvisation produces some of the ensemble textures.

- *Solo characteristics:* Bop and hard bop soloing interspersed with rock figures and rock clichés; heated playing at fast tempos, folk-like playing at slow tempos; some collective improvisation.

- *Rhythm section characteristics:* drummer uses repetitious rock rhythm figures and rock cliché fills interspersed with jazz figures; keeps time in even eighth or sixteenth notes and, if *ostinato* bass line is used, drummer may play ostinato rhythm; bass plays ostinato or intricate walking lines; piano sometimes comps in even eighth-note patterns, sometimes inserting funky melodic ideas; guitar plays rock clichés and patterns.

- *Notable bands:* the Maynard Ferguson Orchestra; the Don Ellis Orchestra; Miles Davis groups; Herbie Hancock groups; Weather Report; Blood, Sweat, and Tears; Chicago; Tom Scott and the L.A. Express; Brecker Brothers; John McLaughlin and the Mahavishnu Orchestra; Matrix; the Crusaders.

- *Performers:*

Trumpet
Miles Davis
Randy Brecker
Don Ellis
Trombone
Jim Pugh

Reeds
Wayne Shorter
Mike Brecker
Tom Scott
Dave Liebman
Bennie Maupin
Joe Farrell

Guitar	Bass
Al Dimeola	Ron Carter
John McLaughlin	Stanley Clarke
Keyboards	Miroslav Vitous
Joe Zawinul	Jaco Pastorius
Chick Corea	
Herbie Hancock	
Drums	
Tony Williams	
Jack DeJohnette	
Billy Cobham	
Billy Hart	
Airto Moreira (Latin American percussion)	

FREE JAZZ (CURRENT)

• *Instrumentation:* May be anything from a solo wind instrument to a large group of mixed rhythm, harmonic, and melodic instruments.

• *Ensemble characteristics:* Improvised interaction is common; may be "spacey" with much electronic distortion and gadgetry, or roots-inspired with heavy percussion, shouts, clapping, whistles, and animal-like horn sounds; a performance is sometimes based on a preset musical premise or sometimes the initial premise is improvised spontaneously; the group may play free of any preset chord frame, free of a preset theme, or free of a time frame containing a regular, recurring pulse.

• *Solo characteristics:* Solos may be remarkably creative but are often self-indulgent, excessive, and repetitious; the most interesting solos are produced by thoughtful, master improvisers.

• *Rhythm section characteristics:* Drummers are able to play at a high energy level without implying a regular pulse and are more involved in a variety of textures than in time keeping; extra percussionists often used for African and South American instruments; bassists skilled at florid, active lines that do not walk in tempo; pianists are very fast, technical, and physical at the keyboard, or they may be lyrical or whimsical.

• *Notable bands:* Sun Ra bands, the Art Ensemble of Chicago, Archie Shepp groups.

- *Performers:*

Trumpet
Don Cherry
Dewey Johnson
Alan Shorter
Randy Brecker
Trombone
Roswell Rudd
Keyboards
Hal Galper
McCoy Tyner
Cecil Taylor
Keith Jarrett
Alto Sax
Ornette Coleman
John Tchicai
Marion Brown
Eric Dolphy
Reeds
Anthony Braxton
Rasaan Roland Kirk

Tenor Sax
Sam Rivers
Albert Ayler
Dewey Redman
Archie Shepp
Mike Brecker
Pharoah Sanders
Drums
Elvin Jones
Billy Higgins
Andrew Cyrille
Bass
Jimmy Garrison
Charles Mingus
Charlie Haden

PIANO STYLES

The history of jazz piano runs parallel to the history of jazz itself, and there are at least four distinct styles: ragtime, stride, boogie woogie, and locked hands.

RAGTIME (ca. 1890–1920)

Ragtime was mostly a piano style, although bands and orchestras at the turn of the century also played rags. And, although ragtime was primarily instrumental, words were sometimes added. A typical ragtime piece would be in $\frac{2}{4}$ meter with a syncopated right-hand melody. This melody would contain stereotyped ragtime rhythms and melodic fragments. The left-hand part would be steady and pulse-like, alternating between single bass notes and chords in the middle register. The single bass notes would be on beats 1 and 3, and the chords would be on beats 2 and 4. The harmonies would be simple and predictable. The effect of the steady left-hand part against the syncopated right-hand melody gave ragtime its jazzy quality, and published rags gave the American public (and Europe) their first heavy exposure to the jazz concept. They were purchased and played by the public to a significant extent. Key composers were Scott Joplin, James Scott, Tom Turpin, and Joseph Lamb.

STRIDE (ca. 1920–1945)

Stride style probably evolved from the left-hand ragtime technique of alternation between low, single notes on beats 1 and 3 and short middle-register chords on beats 2 and 4. The right hand could either comp in syncopation or play a single-note melody. This style was often played at fast tempos in contrast to ragtime, and a lone pianist could simulate an entire rhythm section: a walking bass (the low, single, percussive notes), a piano (the comped chords), a drummer (the combined steady rhythm), and melodic horns (simulated by the right hand). The originator of stride is said to be James P. Johnson, and other well-known pianists who have utilized stride are Willie "The Lion" Smith, Fats Waller, Art Tatum, and Oscar Peterson. Stride became swing-stride and was valid throughout the swing period.

BOOGIE WOOGIE (ca. 1920–1935)

Boogie woogie is a piano style based most often on blues chord changes, and it has had a limited and spotty success as a fad. Its fascination lies mostly in the machine-like rhythm it generates. The typical left-hand pattern is in even eighth-note octave skips, alternating between the small finger and the thumb, so that eight pulses per bar are heard instead of four. Hence the expression, "8 to the bar." This much is like an ostinato figure. Chords and repetitive melodic material are played by the right hand. The originator is said to be Pine Top Smith, and others who have helped to popularize boogie woogie are Meade Lux Lewis, Jimmy Yancy, Albert Ammons, and Pete Johnson.

LOCKED HANDS (ca. 1945–1960)

Locked hands piano style is achieved by moving both hands in the same direction and in the same rhythm, with the hands lying close together and creating a chordal texture instead of a pulsing, rhythmic texture.

The uppermost note in this block chord texture is heard as the melody. The style is often associated with the cool movement, and some important exponents of locked hands style are Milt Buckner, Lennie Tristano, George Shearing, Oscar Peterson, and Bill Evans.

URBAN MUSIC

The history of jazz is linked to urban centers. After its beginnings in New Orleans, jazz also became established in Chicago, Kansas City, New York, and the West Coast, and it began to thrive in many other urban centers throughout the country as well. Jazz became a city music because it was in the large metropolitan areas that jazz musicians were able to find employment, meet other jazz players, and share new concepts.

To some extent, jazz reflects city life. The tempo, the tensions, the noisy, hectic business of life in the city are often apparent in how jazz players interpret the music. The cities nurtured jazz, and because the character of night life varied from city to city, the music was different in each of the influential cities. Since there is no significant night life in rural areas and since night life is essential for musicians, jazz had to become almost entirely an urban music.

CONTEMPORARY STYLES

The newer jazz styles are often a blend or fusion of several different musical influences. The 1970s saw a renewed interest in jazz while at the same time jazz musicians were investigating new means of expression. Some became interested in the Third World and began to use African, Eastern, or South American folk music and native instruments. These elements were fused with jazz techniques. Some musicians fused jazz with rock, as has already been discussed. Some fused jazz with gospel and soul music. Some fused jazz with electronics, synthesizers, odd meters, and other seemingly incongruous elements. In truth, any of these diverse elements are apt to appear in a concert or recording and make jazz sense if the improviser uses them with jazz techniques and in a sensitive manner. Some groups who have used these mixes are listed below:

Jazz rock: The Don Ellis Orchestra; Matrix; the Crusaders; Blood, Sweat and Tears; Chicago; Herbie Hancock; Tom Scott and the L. A. Express; Brecker Brothers; John McLaughlin and the Mahavishnu Orchestra.

Eastern-, African-, or South-American-influenced jazz: The Don Ellis Orchestra; Paul Winter Consort; Keith Jarrett; Anthony Braxton; Miles Davis; Chick Corea; Airto; Gato Barbieri; Chuck Mangione; Santana; Irakere.

Jazz soul: Stevie Wonder; Santana; Joni Mitchell; Marvin Gaye; Grover Washington Jr.

Several of these musicians and groups routinely use electronically boosted instruments and synthesizers as well as traditional folk instruments (percussion, whistles, sitar). European bands have also incorporated many of these diverse sounds.

THE LATIN INFLUENCE

One final kind of music to be mentioned in connection with jazz trends is the music of Latin America. Jazz musicians often generalize all of this music as "Latin," but since the turn of the century, Cuban, South American, and Mexican popular music has influenced American popular music, American dance styles, and American musicians. The American musicians have found the Latin rhythms and percussionists to be particularly irresistible.

Many of these new Latin rhythms arrived in the United States as new dance styles:

1900:	the Habañera
1910–1920s:	the Tango
1930s:	the Rhumba
1940s:	the Conga and the Samba
1950s:	the Mambo and the Cha Cha
1960s:	the Bossa Nova
1970s:	the Salsa

Each of these dance styles is a rhythm style, and the majority of them are of Cuban origin. Additionally, American music has been influenced by Cuban musicians such as the following:

Chano Pozo, conga drummer with Gillespie
Machito, band leader, recorded with Charlie Parker

Pérez Prado, band leader, composer
Mongo Santamaria, leader, percussionist
Chico O'Farrill, composer
Candido, percussionist with Gillespie, Kenton, Herman

One of the newest and most exciting Cuban groups to influence American jazz is Irakere, an explosive band of horns, rhythm instruments, and extra percussionists.

The Latin fusion with American jazz appears to be an ongoing development as well as a healthy, revitalizing influence. And with each passing day, the distinctions between one pure type of music and another become less distinct. We can recognize influences, however, and we can label music as jazz when it relies on the element of improvisation for solo expressiveness within the popular music frame of reference.

SUGGESTED RECORDS:

PHIL WOODS, *Musique du Bois*. Muse MR-5037
SONNY FORTUNE, *Awakening*. A&M Horizon SP-704
RICHIE COLE, *Hollywood Madness*. Muse MR-5207
DON CHERRY, *The Avant-Garde*. Atlantic SD-1451
TED CURSON, *Jubilant Power*. Inner City IC-1017
CHET BAKER, *You Can't Go Home Again*. Horizon SP 726
JOHN COLTRANE, *Blue Train*. BLP 1577
The Smithsonian Collection of Classic Jazz

The Smithsonian Collection is available from The Smithsonian Associates, Washington, D.C. 20560, and from W. W. Norton & Co., Inc., 500 Fifth Avenue, New York, N.Y. 10036.

SUGGESTIONS FOR LISTENING:

1. Using the guides in this chapter and a player from the listening list, try describing a wind instrument player's style.
2. Describe a pianist's style. A bassist's style. A drummer's style.
3. From the record list, choose three trumpet players or three alto saxophonists, and compare them stylistically. (Use the guides.)
4. From the historical record collection, choose two historical period examples, one of which follows the other chronologically, and compare them in detail.

SUGGESTED FURTHER READINGS:

The Jazz Idiom, Jerry Coker; chapter 2.
Jazz City, Leroy Ostransky.
The Jazz Story, Dave Dexter Jr.; chapters 1 to 11.
Understanding Jazz, Leroy Ostransky; chapters 5 to 12.
Jazz Styles, Mark C. Gridley; parts II, III, and IV.
The Jazz Life, Nat Hentoff; chapters 4 and 12.
Jazz: A History, Frank Tirro; Transcriptions, pp. 365–386, and chapters 6 to 13.
Jazz Style in Kansas City and the Southwest, Ross Russell.
The American Dance Band Discography, Brian Rust (lists every dance band recording from 1917 to 1942).
The Big Bands (revised edition), George T. Simon.
The Story of Jazz, Marshall W. Stearns; parts IV and V, chapters 20 and 21.
Jazz: The Transition Years, John S. Wilson.

CHAPTER EIGHT

IMPORTANT INNOVATORS AND STYLE SETTERS

Following a study of the jazz history outline, one could reasonably be confused about which personalities are significant. Who are the important people, and why?

What follows is a collection of important innovators with an explanation of why jazz researchers deem the contributions by these individuals to be significant. They are grouped according to their instruments, or as band leaders.

Naturally, when such a list of superstars is compiled, well-known favorites will sometimes be omitted. The intent of this listing is to name musicians who have made meaningful contributions to jazz as an art form. Polls, gold records, publicity hype, and talk show appearances do not necessarily place an artist in that category.

TRUMPET

LOUIS ARMSTRONG (1900–1971)

The first jazz artist to receive worldwide attention was Louis Armstrong. His trumpet style influenced all subsequent trumpet players with its directness, simplicity, warmth, and swing feeling. Many jazz historians rate Armstrong as the single greatest jazz man. His playing had rhythmic drive and excitement, and he was perhaps the first to play jazz solos that were truly virtuosic, with a sense of form and drama. He was also one of the first "hot" players to record prolifically and, as a result, he was especially influential. His playing was studied and imitated throughout the world.

DIZZY GILLESPIE (1917—   )

A superb musician, Dizzy Gillespie is usually credited, along with Charlie Parker, with being a major creative force in the bop period, which redefined melody, harmony, and rhythm for jazz players. He made technique a part of the new jazz, so that those who followed him were obliged to develop their technical ability to a greater degree than was previously necessary for jazz trumpet. Gillespie's dazzling facility and novel melodic ideas continue to be inspirational for jazz trumpeters.

MILES DAVIS (1926—   )

As a young man, Miles Davis worked with Parker and Gillespie as a bop trumpeter on many recordings and club dates. He then became a major force in the cool movement as a leader and player, and he developed a lyrical and delicate melodic style that was the basis for many popular, top-selling albums. A major achievement has been Davis's advancement of modal compositions to replace those with complex chord changes. Consequently, many jazz players reorganized their improvisational techniques in order to accommodate modal structures.

TROMBONE

JACK TEAGARDEN (1905–1964)

Before the arrival of the mature Jack Teagarden on the jazz scene of the 1920s, there was no well-defined jazz trombone style. Teagarden's playing was greatly admired and imitated, and he brought the trombone out of its secondary role in the Dixie ensemble and into its own as a powerful solo voice. He made jazz trombone a driving, expressive idiom with his big, wholesome tone and with technique to accommodate inspired improvisation.

BILL HARRIS (1916–1973)

Bill Harris created a style model for trombone that was imitated by many players in the 1940s and 1950s. The tone was wide and meaty with an individualistic vibrato on slow tunes. At fast tempos, Harris's solos were made up of unique rhythmic figures, glisses, and shouts, and the jazz drive was always logical and clear. He was thought to be the strongest brass soloist in the Woody Herman band of the 1940s.

J. J. JOHNSON (1924—   )

Of the many trombonists who were active during the bop period, J. J. Johnson seems to have had the greatest impact. He may have been the first to successfully adapt the trombone to the speedy bop style. His improvised playing was fast and clean, and it was assumed by many that he was playing a valve trombone and not a slide trombone. The J. J. Johnson style was imitated by many trombonists during the 1950s, further advancing melodic agility and rapid technique for the instrument.

ALTO SAXOPHONE

JOHNNY HODGES (1906–1970)

As the jazz alto player with Ellington for longer than anyone else, Johnny Hodges received worldwide acclaim for his swinging jazz style. He later concentrated on a slow melodic ballad style using his velvety smooth tone and sweeping, slow glisses. His relaxed approach to the alto sax made Hodges, along with Benny Carter, the alto sax player to emulate in the 1930s.

CHARLIE PARKER (1920–1955)

Charlie Parker was the key figure in the bop movement who caused all jazz players to reevaluate improvised melody, rhythm, and chords. He was a virtuoso whose consistency and quality level never faltered. Parker was one of the most creative jazz soloists ever, and his improvisations are still being analyzed, memorized, orchestrated, and imitated. He initiated a new school of saxophone playing, and his influence can be heard in all modern sax players.

SOPRANO SAXOPHONE

SIDNEY BECHET (1897–1959)

The only soprano saxophonist to maintain an artist's stature with the instrument until modern times, Sidney Bechet became a beloved national figure in France and lived in Paris from the late 1940s until his death. He was a well-known jazz player from his youth in New Orleans, where he began playing with Freddie Keppard and Bunk Johnson (ca. 1912), to the 1950s. Bechet played in a florid style with a wide vibrato, and his individualistic melody making was moving and warm.

JOHN COLTRANE (1926–1967)

A virtuosic tenor saxophonist (see below), John Coltrane was also influential in reviving interest in the soprano saxophone. He began using it in addition to the tenor sax in 1960, and it quickly caught on as a jazz instrument again. By the 1970s, jazz saxophonists such as Sonny Rollins, Cannonball Adderly, Joe Farrell, and Dave Liebman were using the soprano sax extensively. It is currently a very popular instrument because of Coltrane, and it is a common double for most alto and tenor saxophonists. Coltrane claimed that playing the soprano sax caused him to reevaluate the low register of the tenor sax. Part of the soprano's popularity is due to its shrill character, which allows it to be heard over loud brass and drums, and its tone quality blends well with electric guitar and electronic keyboards.

TENOR SAXOPHONE

COLEMAN HAWKINS (1904–1969)

The first to concentrate on tenor saxophone as a jazz instrument, Coleman Hawkins became the father of tenor sax playing, sustaining a worldwide reputation from his early days with Fletcher Henderson (1923) into the bop period. He maintained his artist's status because he was a virtuoso improviser, developing elaborate lines from the harmonic aspects of a tune, and his ornate style and husky tone were imitated by all of his swing period competitors. Even into the twilight of his long career, the Hawkins sound was intense and gripping, and his imaginative improvising was undiminished.

LESTER YOUNG (1909–1959)

The advent of Lester Young inspired a new tenor sax sound—a light, clear tone instead of a dark, throaty one, a slow vibrato instead of a fast vibrato—and a new way of thinking out a melody which was a model of uncluttered improvising. His melodic thinking seemed to prove the saying, "Less is more." Although he was pre-bop, many bop tenor players such as Zoot Sims, Stan Getz, and Allen Eager have emulated him. He also inspired altoist Charlie Parker. These younger musicians were especially impressed by Young's phrasing, which, instead of falling into symmetrical 4-bar phrases, was apt to spin out in long, smooth lines of unpredictable length, forecasting the style of improvisation which was to come in the bop period. Young was at his best during the years he spent with Count Basie prior to World War II.

JOHN COLTRANE (1926–1967)

As with Charlie Parker, John Coltrane's playing was thought-provoking. He always presented the listener with the strong impression that there was a serious mind at work behind the horn. Unlike Parker, however, Coltrane was a much more technical player, and this caused some listeners to hear only a steady stream of scales. He was, in fact, wrenching as much melody as possible from each chord of a tune. The process was more compelling because of his searing tone and intensity. He worked, as Coleman Hawkins did, from the harmonic changes in a composition, but the results were breathtaking because of the heat and speed at which he played. There were very few pauses in a Coltrane solo, and this added further to the intensity. Nearly all of the technically fast reed soloists heard today owe a debt to Coltrane's genius.

Mention must also be made of Coltrane's compositions, which are examples of pure jazz writing containing few concessions to commercialism. His compositions fall into three general categories: the jazz-modal tunes such as "Impressions" and "Naima"; the many blues-structured pieces such as "Cousin Mary," "Bessie's Blues," and "Equinox"; and a third group of more unusual compositions such as "Moment's Notice" and the radical "Giant Steps." Many of these tunes have been recorded by other jazz stars and bands, and a few such as "Giant Steps" and "Naima" have become true jazz classics.

BARITONE SAXOPHONE

HARRY CARNEY (1910–1974)

The baritone saxophonist with Duke Ellington for more than forty years, Harry Carney became the first to win fame as a jazz soloist on this unlikely looking instrument. It is believed that much of the special flavor of the Ellington sound derived from Carney's tone quality in the sax section. His improvisations were logical and vigorous, with a rich, fat tone, and for decades he was practically the only great virtuoso on the baritone sax.

GERRY MULLIGAN (1927—   )

Gerry Mulligan was the instrumentalist most responsible for bringing the baritone sax into contemporary focus. His improvising was cool and direct, and his playing was so delicate and smooth that he gave one the fleeting impression that he might be playing an alto instead of a baritone sax. Mulligan's tone is still light and dry, and his melody making is warm and romantic on slow ballads and relaxed and thoughtful on up-tempo tunes. He also continues to be an original, creative arranger and composer.

CLARINET

BENNY GOODMAN (1909—   )

When one is asked to name a prominent jazz clarinetist, it is probably Benny Goodman who first comes to mind. Although he is well-known for being the leader of one of the most famous swing bands, his personal musicianship cannot be overlooked. His tone was clear and refined, and his technique was flawless. On slow ballads he played the melody in paraphrase, and with medium or fast tunes he swung hard, building jazz lines from syncopated chord arpeggiation and scale fragments. His bright, driving style sent all aspiring swing clarinetists back to the etudes and scale books in order to be able to "play like Goodman."

PIANO

JAMES P. JOHNSON (1891–1955)

Considered the father of the stride piano style, James P. Johnson combined ragtime piano techniques with horn-like drive and ensemble-like power. Johnson was a New York musician whose stride style was adopted by others such as Fats Waller, Willie "The Lion" Smith, and Art Tatum.

ART TATUM (1910–1956)

A man gifted with breathtaking technique, Art Tatum was skilled in reharmonizing well-known standard tunes to give them a fresh sound. He could be original and lucid at very fast tempos and still swing nicely, and he was fond of inserting quotes from other melodies in the midst of dazzling jazz lines. Tatum worked as a soloist or with a small combo, and although his recordings do not do him full justice, they are amazing even by today's standards.

BUD POWELL (1924–1966)

Bud Powell developed a new type of comping which was fragmented and irregular with regard to the pulse, and a solo style which contained the technique and speed to match the bop horn players with whom he performed. Powell's improvisations were very forceful and rhythmically surprising, and his influence on jazz pianists of the 1940s and 1950s was quite apparent.

BILL EVANS (1929–1980)

After playing with Miles Davis for a short time, Bill Evans recorded with a trio and, during this period, his keyboard concepts were distilled and confirmed. Evolving from a bop style, his technique featured a sustained left hand with modal inferences and a right hand that often played clusters of adjacent notes. He also favored the locked hands style of chording parallel to the improvised melody. He created melodic inventions that were smooth and graceful, with rhythmic freshness and surprise.

THELONIOUS MONK (1920–1982)

Along with Parker and Gillespie, Thelonious Monk was a key figure in the bop period of jazz. He will probably be remembered more for his composing than for his pianistic skills. As a jazz pianist, Monk was inventive and eccentric, playing melodic lines that were often angular and tension-filled. He would employ abrupt silent spots in his playing, repeat an oddly voiced chord several times in order to create suspense before moving on, or utilize a single repeated note for a similar purpose. He would also cease comping for a period of time and allow the soloist to continue without the piano.

As a composer, Monk produced some of the most singular pieces of the bop period, some of which became evergreens. They were truly original and yet simple and logical, and the list includes ballads, standard 32-bar jazz pieces, and blues-derived pieces. Some are " 'Round Midnight," "Misterioso," "Straight, No Chaser," "Well, You Needn't," "Epistrophy," "In Walked Bud," "Nutty," "Blue Monk," "Rhythm-A-Ning," and "I Mean You."

BASS

JIMMY BLANTON (1921–1942)

Recognized as the first to move the string bass beyond its early position as simply a pulse instrument that delivered a steady stream of quarter notes, Jimmy Blanton developed the bass as a melodic instrument as well. He was a pioneer in jazz bass improvisation, and although he played with Duke Ellington for only two years (1939–1941) before leaving because of illness, Blanton's technical virtuosity, rhythmic drive, and tone affected all serious jazz bassists who were to develop in the next several decades.

OSCAR PETTIFORD (1922—   )

Inspired by Blanton, Oscar Pettiford became one of the bassists most in demand in the bop period. A skilled improviser, he furthered technical agility on the instrument, and this, coupled with melodic inventiveness, gradually became the norm in a jazz bass solo. A by-product of this virtuosity was that recording engineers became more aware of the bass and began to record it more carefully than before.

MIROSLAV VITOUS (1947—   )

The bassist with the original Weather Report, Miroslav Vitous developed, with Joe Zawinul and Wayne Shorter, new roles for the modern jazz bassist in collective improvisation. His bass did not simply walk or solo, but also conversed with, commented on, and interjected itself into the ever-changing textures this group created as they explored a piece of music. Vitous could bow a horn-like line or play a rock line, but his greater contribution lay in his role in the fluid improvised textures of the group.

DRUMS

GENE KRUPA (1909–1973)

Gene Krupa probably did more than anyone else to popularize the idea of the solo jazz drummer. While he was with Goodman, the band recorded several pieces that featured extended jazz drum solos. These solos were comprised mostly of drum rudiments and were nearly always played in time, but they were flashy and exciting when seen live and set the standard for the big jazz band drum solo. In becoming so visible, Krupa also helped set the norm for a standard drum set consisting of a bass drum with foot pedal, hi-hat cymbal with foot pedal, snare drum, ride cymbal, crash cymbal, and tom-toms.

KENNY CLARKE (1914—   )

Along with Max Roach, Kenny Clarke initiated the changes that were to occur in the drummer's role in the rhythm section. These alterations became apparent during the development of bop and involved transforming the drummer from a mere time keeper to an accompanist who keeps time, comments, accents, and fills with the ensemble and the soloist. Clarke is generally credited with the idea of keeping time on the ride cymbal rather than on the hi-hat cymbal and snare drum, as the swing drummers did.

ELVIN JONES (1927—   )

Elvin Jones became influential while performing with Coltrane and continues to be studied by most serious jazz drummers. Seemingly inspired by African drum ensembles, he successfully performs several different rhythms simultaneously (*polyrhythms*) on the drum set while at the same time accompanying with a loose sort of time that is present but not rigid. His polyrhythmic style is powerful and imaginative as it swells and subsides with changing textures and colors. Jones has moved the jazz drummer beyond time keeping and filling and into a role as an equal improvisational partner in the jazz combo.

GUITAR

CHARLIE CHRISTIAN (1919–1942)

Charlie Christian is generally credited with establishing the jazz guitar soloist as a normal element in jazz presentations. Previously, the jazz ensemble guitar was mainly a rhythm instrument. If the player did solo, the solos were chord-structured. Christian soloed with long melodic lines, and the guitar was heard because he was one of the first to use electric amplification. It is tragic that he died only two years after joining Benny Goodman. There are only a few recordings that show his inventiveness and contemporary ideas, and one can only speculate on the manner in which he influenced jazz performance.

KENNY BURRELL (1931—)
AND WES MONTGOMERY (1925–1968)

Both Kenny Burrell and Wes Montgomery became known during the hard bop period when they played and recorded with such stars as John Coltrane, Sonny Rollins, Hank Jones, Ron Carter, Percy Heath, and Tommy Flanagan. Burrell was apt to be more funky while Montgomery was usually in swing drive producing tasty ideas, often in guitar octaves. Both men were playing a valid jazz style of guitar, incorporating much melodic originality, at a time when a profusion of rock guitarists were substituting electronics for imagination.

VIBRAPHONE

LIONEL HAMPTON (1913—)

Reputed to be the first to make the vibes an accepted jazz instrument, Lionel Hampton was with the Goodman band and the Goodman quartet for several years. It was during this time that his impact was greatest. His technique, polish, and touch were dazzling, and he matched Goodman note for note at top speeds. At slow tempos he played warm, lovely melodies which demonstrated the glowing possibilities of the vibraphone. Following this period Hampton became a successful big band leader in his own right.

MILT JACKSON (1923—)

Widely known for his excellent work with the Modern Jazz Quartet, Milt Jackson was first known as a premier bop stylist performing with such musicians as Dizzy Gillespie, Tad Dameron, and Thelonious Monk. His playing was less flashy than Hampton's, and he stroked the bars in a controlled manner. Jackson used much less vibrato (slower tremolo speed) and produced melodic ideas that were subtle and cool yet interesting and inventive. His solos swung nicely but all was neat and carefully phrased.

GARY BURTON (1943—)

Gary Burton has recorded solo and duo (with piano), and has played with George Shearing and with groups whose styles range from bop to jazz-rock to avant-garde. His vibraphone skills are phenomenal. He has learned how to bend tones, has developed a stick system for a new way to handle chromaticism on the vibes keyboard, and regularly uses four mallets in order to accompany himself so that one can hear melody, harmony, and counterpoint simultaneously. Burton's new sophisticated techniques have made his playing sensitive and unique without a trace of contrivance.

BAND LEADERS

DUKE ELLINGTON (1899–1974)

It is not possible in this study to list all of the composing and scoring innovations first used by Duke Ellington. In the fifty-some years in which he kept his orchestra together as an organic whole, he invented instrumental voicings, colors, and combinations that were both striking and practical for the jazz band. He was known for using the personal playing characteristics of particular soloists in his orchestrations. He also composed over 1000 pieces, many of which were set with lyrics to become standards in the American pop music repertoire. Without the constancy of the Ellington orchestra, ever present from the 1920s to the 1970s, and without the brilliance of Ellington himself, American music and jazz in particular would not be what it is today.

COUNT BASIE (1904—   )

The Count Basie band is the ideal model for a demonstration of big band swing. For nearly forty-five years (since 1937), the Count Basie band has been a continuous force in jazz, producing superb players, classic scores, and a sound that neophyte bands attempt to emulate. It is generally believed that the Basie rhythm section is responsible for the relaxed swing feeling that the band imparts, and although the personnel has, of course, changed through the years, the swing qualities have been continued by the replacements. Arrangers who have added to the Basie library include Sammy Nestico, Neal Hefti, Thad Jones, Frank Foster, Quincy Jones, and Benny Carter. Also adding to the Basie band's excellence was the inspired soloing of players such as Lester Young, Wardell Gray, Don Byas, Eddie "Lockjaw" Davis,

Frank Foster, Clark Terry, Thad Jones, Snooky Young, Jo Jones, and Louis Bellson.

BENNY GOODMAN (1909—   )

As leader of the band which, because of a weekly NBC radio show in 1935, made the public aware of swing and big band music, Benny Goodman achieved instant recognition. Subsequent public appearances and recordings, many of which featured arrangements by Fletcher Henderson, placed Goodman on the cutting edge of the swing era, and he maintained his reputation and popularity until he chose to retire in the mid-1940s. He has periodically organized bands since that time, but his activities as a leader have been limited. He was an uncompromising musician in several ways: he was a dazzling jazz clarinetist who expected and received excellent performances from his players; he led a band that always played in swing style, and, whether the tune was a standard or popular song of the day, the band and the arrangement made few concessions to commercialism; and his was the first band to seriously go about integrating superior black musicians into a basically white band. In addition to scores of admirable white musicians, Goodman used outstanding black musicians such as Teddy Wilson, Lionel Hampton, Cootie Williams, Trummy Young, Wardell Gray, Fletcher Henderson, Charlie Christian, Sid Catlett, and Slam Stewart.

WOODY HERMAN (1913—   )

Another uncompromising leader who held his band together through poor economic periods, Woody Herman has consistently updated his library with new arrangements and compositions by talented writers. Leading a band almost constantly since the late 1930s, Herman and his successive groups evolved with the trends, changing from early blues-based swing to today's jazz-rock. The Herman band has been a showcase for arrangers such as Neal Hefti, Ralph Burns, and Alan Broadbent and for superb soloists such as Stan Getz, Flip Phillips, Zoot Sims, Gene Ammons, Conte Candoli, Urbie Green, Bill Harris, Milt Jackson, and Dave Tough.

STAN KENTON (1912–1979)

The Stan Kenton bands were big in size and in sound. Using large brass sections, often including tuba and French horns, pitted against a small reed section, the sound could be intense, Wagnerian, solemn, and pretentious. But it is also true that when the band was swinging it was an irresistible force that could be felt physically. The Kenton band featured complex scores containing rich harmonies and counterpoint, and Kenton encouraged arrangers such as Russ García, Pete Rugolo, Bill Russo, Dee Barton, Bill Holman, Johnny Richards, and Hank Levy to write ambitious compositions for the band. Many of these scores were recorded and published through Kenton's own Creative World corporation. He actively promoted the band and had a large following among high school and college big band fans, and he is significant in this regard because of his fervent belief in and personal commitment to jazz education. Kenton and his entire band participated in high school and college jazz clinics, festivals, and in-residence jazz camps across the country. Because of Kenton's belief in youth and the jazz heritage, thousands of youngsters have been inspired and instructed by professional jazz musicians. His unselfishness was exceptional and his influence on jazz education inestimable.

DON ELLIS (1934–1979)

Don Ellis must be listed here because of his serious commitment to the exploration of new ideas and new idioms for the big band concept. Beyond the fact that he was an exciting jazz trumpeter, he was interested in new means of expressiveness for the large jazz ensemble. His bands swung and soloists improvised in nonsymmetrical meters such as $\frac{5}{4}, \frac{5}{8}, \frac{7}{4}, \frac{7}{8}, \frac{11}{4}$, etc. In addition, the piece would be likely to contain a rock identity through the inclusion of a rock bass line and chord progression. Ellis often incorporated into his scores an amplified string quartet, two drum set drummers, and a conga drummer. At times he also used traditional instruments from India such as the sitar and the tabla. Indian melody was often used and this led to microtonal or quarter-tone tuning and playing and to the development of a quarter-tone trumpet, on which Ellis soloed. The individuals in the reed section were sometimes tuned within quarter tones of each other. Eastern, Indian, and African influences were fused with rock structures, and all was distorted, amplified, loop-delayed, and synthesized with many types of live electronics. All these elements seemed to coalesce and produce stimulating jazz because of Ellis's inspired leadership. His bands were truly remarkable and his musicianship was brilliant.

SUGGESTED RECORDS:

From *The Smithsonian Collection of Classic Jazz,* solos by Louis Armstrong, Dizzy Gillespie, Miles Davis, J. J. Johnson, Johnny Hodges with Ellington, Charlie Parker, Sidney Bechet, Coleman Hawkins, Lester Young, Benny Goodman, James P. Johnson, Art Tatum, Bud Powell, Thelonious Monk, Jimmy Blanton with Ellington, Elvin Jones with John Coltrane, Charlie Christian, Lionel Hampton.

DON ELLIS, *Electric Bath.* Columbia CS-9585

SUGGESTIONS FOR LISTENING:

1. This chapter names some famous innovators and style setters who were imitated to some degree by many others. Using the criteria for innovation or style setting, who would you add to the list? Can you justify their inclusion?
2. Thelonious Monk, although most individualistic, might not have been listed as a style setter. Can you determine why?
3. Some alto saxophonists who have been heard in recordings cited earlier owe a stylistic debt to Charlie Parker. Can you name them?
4. Some tenor saxophonists who have been heard in recordings cited earlier owe a stylistic debt to John Coltrane. Can you name them?
5. Some trumpet players who have been heard in recordings cited earlier owe a stylistic debt to Dizzy Gillespie. Can you name them?

SUGGESTED FURTHER READINGS:

The New Edition of the Encyclopedia of Jazz, Leonard Feather.
The Encyclopedia of Jazz in the Sixties, Leonard Feather.
The Encyclopedia of Jazz in the Seventies, Leonard Feather.

Jazz: A History, Frank Tirro; Transcriptions, p. 365.
The Jazz Life, Nat Hentoff; Epilogue, p. 249.
Hear Me Talkin' to Ya, Nat Shapiro and Nat Hentoff, eds.; chapters 19 and 20.
Who's Who of Jazz, John Chilton.
Jazz Masters in Transition, 1957–69, Martin Williams.
Black Giants, Pauline Rivelli and Robert Levin, eds.; interviews.

EVALUATING JAZZ IMPROVISERS

HISTORICAL DEVELOPMENT OF IMPROVISATION

The history of jazz and the development of jazz improvisation are inseparable. In early New Orleans jazz, the original melody was preeminent and the improviser simply hung *elaborations* on this tune. It was not that the players were not adventurous, but more likely that they simply felt that the original tune should be recognizable. In the early swing era, the player ornamented the tune and also "ragged" the melody, causing it to be syncopated and rhythmically irregular. This was a kind of melodic paraphrasing and the tune was often still recognizable.

Later in the swing era, the original melody had all but disappeared from an improvised solo, and the player used the underlying *chords* from the original tune as a basis for the improvisation. These chords were arpeggiated in various ways, and this chordal improvising is called "running the changes." The arpeggiated chords were also combined with scalar materials and melody fragments by the more imaginative players.

In the bop period which followed, the improvisations were still chord-oriented, but there was much made of *chord alterations* to maintain interest. Jazz from this period often contains complete reharmonizations of the original composition as well as substitute chords, altered chords, and enriched chords of all descriptions.

In music from the hard bop period and beyond, *chord scales* began to be used in solos. Chord scales were not uncommon in earlier periods, but at this later time there was a conscious effort to use them heavily. Chord scales are scales which, when played against a given chord, sound compatible with it. Their use came about partly because of the new attraction to limited modal harmony. This caused the player to try to expand what could be done within such a limitation without becoming repetitious. It was also at about this time that *patterns* of all descriptions became more important. One can often hear an improviser from this period using an intricate pattern which ascends or descends in sequence through a passage of several measures.

And so, through the history of jazz, the solo style has developed from elaboration of the melody, to "ragging" the melody, to arpeggiating the chords, to using chord alterations, to the use of chord scales and patterns. Today's resourceful jazz soloist can and does utilize all these techniques at various times.

THE IMPROVISER AS COMPOSER

Improvisation is the paramount factor that separates jazz from other musical activities. Jazz is the only kind of music in which the player is expected to be creative to any significant extent in the performance of the original material. Improvisation is a set of skills which jazz musicians are supposed to be able to produce when needed.

Each day, in every state in the nation, thousands of student musicians are taking lessons on piano, guitar, band, and orchestral instruments. Yet they are not, except rarely, given improvisation instruction. It is not a required proficiency for playing marching band, concert band, orchestral, or piano music. Accomplished improvisation is only occasionally required in rock music. If some of these musicians become interested in playing jazz, they soon discover that they are beginners again as improvisers. An entirely new set of skills must be learned, practiced, and mastered before they can fully enjoy playing this music and being accepted by other jazz musicians.

Jazz, and indeed all music, exists in time. Thus, the jazz improviser must organize his or her material to make a coherent musical statement in time—the length of time in which it exists. The painter and the sculptor work with the visual image. Dance and film, although they are processes in a time frame, also depend upon the visual image for expressiveness. The improviser (composer) works only with sound organized in time.

An excellent comparison of composer and improviser, with probing insights into the way the improviser assembles his ideas, may be found in the following excerpt from an article by Malcolm E. Bessom which appeared in the *Music Educators Journal:*

Composing and improvising are alike and different. One obvious difference is that a composer writes down his or her music for someone else to perform, whereas an improviser compresses the creation and re-creation processes into a single, simultaneous act. Another obvious difference is that a composer consciously deliberates over his choice of notes. He writes and revises, and revises again, until he is convinced that each note on the page is the best possible choice at that particular point. An improviser does not have that opportunity for revision; he or she hopes that the first choice of notes is the best choice because one cannot stop in mid-performance and say, "Let me try that last phrase one more time."

Most people perceive these differences, but beyond that they think of composing and improvising as murky, mysterious subjects. They call forth that marvelous word "inspiration" to explain away the creative act as something that perhaps even the artist should not understand. It is supposedly like a divine communication extended to a chosen few who accept it without question. Actually, there are better words to substitute for "inspiration"—among them "work," "study," "knowledge," "experience," "perception," and "mental activity."

Both improvising and composing are controlled mental activities based on training and experience, and both draw on knowledge that lies at the surface of the mind or deep in its recesses. Like an actor who works for years to become known as an "overnight success," the composer and improviser study, accumulate a wealth of technical knowledge and understanding, practice, woodshed their ideas and techniques, and pay their professional dues in order to write or perform a few notes that listeners will call an "inspiration." For an improviser, it's a matter of getting it all together in order to know what to do next when the opportunity arises. When the moment comes, the musician pulls together his or her act: he consciously thinks through some of the things he plays or sings; he subconsciously lets his fingers run through a chord or figure or phrase that he has played hundreds of times before and doesn't need to concentrate on; he draws from a mental storehouse of musical ideas he has heard and tried and practiced and some that he has never before tried; he calls upon his experience to tell him what to leave out as well as what to put in; and he consciously works out his approach to putting all these elements together into a meaningful expression. He joins intellect with intuition.

Igor Stravinsky called composing "selective improvisation." One might think, then, that improvising is nonselective composition, but that's not true. An improviser also selects, in a knowing way. And though it is seemingly instant composition, improvisation is instant only in the sense of making a final decision, a string of final decisions, during performance. Those decisions are considered ones, based on years of thought, waiting only for the right moment to take shape and find expression.

The late clarinetist Pee Wee Russell told critic Whitney Balliett (in Balliett's book *Such Sweet Thunder*) about some of the things that went through his mind while improvising: "You take each solo like it was the last one you were going to play in your life. What notes to hit, and when to hit them—that's the secret. You can *make* a particular phrase with just one note. Maybe at the end, maybe at the beginning. It's like a little pattern. What will lead in quietly and not be too emphatic. Sometimes I jump the right chord and use what seems wrong to the next guy but I *know* is right for me. I usually think about four bars ahead what I am going to play. Sometimes things go wrong, and I have to scramble. . . . In lots of cases, your solo depends on who you're following. The guy played a great chorus, you say to yourself. How am I going to follow *that?* I applaud him inwardly, and it becomes a matter of silent pride. Not jealousy, mind you. A kind of competition. So I make myself a guinea pig—what the hell, I'll try something new. All this goes through your mind in a split second."

Creativity takes time—years, months, a few days, and a split second to complete the product. It depends on how you perceive what is involved in improvisation or composition. All this, of course, does not guarantee a quality product. Handel turned out his entire *Messiah* in just twenty-four days, and it has lived for 200 years. But another composer may spend a year or more making decisions on what notes to use in what order, and the result may not be worth five minutes' reflection. Similarly, an improviser may make final decisions from moment to moment and, because it is spontaneous, elicit amazement from an unknowing listener. But possibly the decisions may call forth only a bunch of clichés—or he or she may come up with some good ideas but be so anxious to get them all out that they become a jumble. Saxophonist Sidney Bechet observed that "there are lots of otherwise good musicians who sound terrible because they start a new idea without finishing the last one." Those who make unique, coherent, artistic choices with some consistency—whether from second to second or, through strictly conscious deliberation, over a longer period of time—are relatively few.[1]

As Bessom has stated, the improviser is spontaneously composing. This fact is effectively brought out in the following excerpt from *Musician, Player & Listener,* in which Zan Stewart is interviewing the tenor saxophonist Johnny Griffin:

MUSICIAN: How do you keep in such good shape (at 50 Griffin is incredibly trim and vital, like a man twenty years younger)?

GRIFFIN: I like feeling good and I just do what my body tells me. You see, music is my life, that's all I know. I've got one path to go down and it has nothing to do with anybody else. I want to play that horn. My days are spent looking forward to that bandstand. That's the pulpit. Everything else is incidental. And it takes no special effort. It's my work and it's my hobby: music. It's just that simple. Music is everything. I think music goes further than any other art form, because I think you're so limited with words. And words, especially in the English language, can have double meanings, so it's hard to tell if somebody's being straight. And with the inflection of the voice, words change meanings. But, you can't lie with music. It's out there. It leaves you naked. Your soul is naked.

MUSICIAN: Painters are naked, too, in that respect. And really anybody that can conjure up images with words.

GRIFFIN: But to be spontaneous, baby. I mean, painting takes time.

MUSICIAN: Yeah, as far as spontaneity goes, there's nothing like jazz.

GRIFFIN: Well, you see, jazz music is special because, at least the way that I dig it, it's a self-expression, and it's not last night, it's today. When Bird said "Now's the Time," it's now. It's not what you played last night or on a record, it's what you're playing . . . [emphatically] now! It's an accumulation of your life up until . . . now! Jazz! That's for me what jazz is. It's how the audience is affecting you now, not yesterday. That's what makes it so exciting for me, because I can play the same tune forever and it never turns out the same way.[2]

MELODIC EXPRESSION

Melody is the basis for musical thought. When a jazz soloist "says something," communicates a musical thought, he or she does so through melodic expression even if performing on an instrument capable of sounding chords. So a piano, guitar, or vibes solo is primarily comprised of melodic ideas (although supported by harmony) just as a trumpet, sax, or flute solo is melodic. Serious jazz students therefore must study and memorize the common building blocks of melody making: scales, arpeggiated chords, sequence, melodic formulas and patterns, and many, many tunes.

The jazz improviser uses the following (see figures 9.1-9.8):

1. Original melody
2. Ornamented original melody
3. Paraphrase of original melody
4. Melody fragments
5. Melodic patterns in sequence
6. Arpeggiated chords
7. Scales and scale fragments
8. Borrowed melodies (quotes)

FIGURE 9.1.

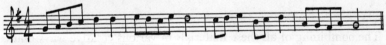

ORIGINAL MELODY

FIGURE 9.2.

ORNAMENTED ORIGINAL MELODY

FIGURE 9.3.

JAZZ PARAPHRASE

FIGURE 9.4.

NEW FRAGMENT   ORIGINAL FRAGMENT

FIGURE 9.5.

PATTERN IN SEQUENCE

FIGURE 9.6.

ARPEGGIATED CHORDS

FIGURE 9.7.

SCALES AND SCALE FRAGMENTS

FIGURE 9.8.

A BORROWED FRAGMENT

The combining of all these materials in various creative ways marks the difference between an ordinary player and a remarkable one. The following are Nat Hentoff's observations in *The Jazz Life* regarding Miles Davis and his feelings about melodic emphasis:

> Davis has made maximum use of his assets. He plays with a burnished tone that can be more expressive in the lower register than that of any of the modernists; and his general musical conception and temperament are annealed to a spare style that fits well with the fact that his technique is somewhat limited.

> Davis has an exceptionally keen and subtle chord sense but his avoidance of bobsledding through changes is due less to his technical limitations than to his increasing concern with melodic improvisation. Davis has come to prefer a minimum of chords in most compositions. "When you go that way, you can go on forever. You don't have to worry about changes and you can do more with the line. It becomes a challenge to see how melodically inventive you are. When you're based on chords, you know at the end of thirty-two bars that

the chords have run out and there's nothing to do but repeat what you've just done—with variations. I think there is a return in jazz to emphasis on melodic rather than harmonic variation. There will be fewer chords but infinite possibilities as to what to do with them. Of course, several classical composers have been writing this way for years. Too much modern jazz became thick with chords."[3]

It is interesting to observe how the common pop music lead sheet reflects melodic thinking. The publisher provides the melody with lyrics below it and chord symbols printed above each measure. The chord symbols represent the supporting harmony. Melody is predominant and harmony assumes a secondary role for jazz expressiveness.

AFFECTIVE FACTORS

Many factors affect a player's solo or the outcome of an attempted solo. Some of these are *tone quality* (bright, dark, smooth, husky, vibrato, no vibrato); *degree of aggressiveness* (player attacks the solo vigorously or is cautious and tentative); *how the player operates in time* (where musical ideas and accents are placed with reference to the fundamental beat); *quickness of technique* (how fast and sure the fingers and hands can move); *reaction speed* (speed with which the player can react to an idea produced by someone else and produce a parallel or complementing idea); *the influence of other players* (their performance may be inspiring or dispiriting); and, finally, an understanding of *listener's expectations.*

It is very helpful for the performer to have some idea as to how people listen to music. How does the performer grab the listener? Keep the listener's attention span at a high level? Keep boredom at a low level? How does the player use improvisational materials to advantage? How does he or she use the listener's background to advantage? Some revealing test results on the subject of listeners' expectations are found in Jerry Coker's book, *Improvising Jazz:*

> Successive, or at least well-placed, variations of motifs, when employed by the jazz improviser, have a definite, strengthening effect upon the relationship between the performer and the listener. Richmond Browne, jazz pianist and instructor of theory at Yale University, wrote in a letter to the author:
>
>> What is the soloist doing when he attempts to "build"? Actually the ideal process hardly ever takes place—that is, it is hardly ever the case that a conscientious soloist plays a thinking solo for

a hard-listening hearer—but when this does happen, the key process is memory. The soloist has to establish for the listener what the important *point*, the motif if you like, is, and then show as much as he can of what it is that he sees in that motif, extending the relationships of it to the basic while never giving the feeling he has forgotten it. In other words, I believe that it should be a basic principle to use repetition, rather than variety—but not too much. The listener is constantly making predictions; actual infinitesimal predictions as to whether the next event will be a repetition of something, or something different. The player is constantly either confirming or denying these predictions in the listener's mind. As nearly as we can tell (Kraehenbuehl at Yale and I), the listener must come out right about 50% of the time—if he is too successful in predicting, he will be bored; if he is too unsuccessful, he will give up and call the music "disorganized."

Thus if the player starts a repetitive pattern, the listener's attention drops away as soon as he has successfully predicted that it is going to continue. Then, if the thing keeps going, the attention curve comes back up, and the listener becomes interested in just how long the pattern *is* going to continue. Similarly, if the player never repeats anything, no matter how tremendous an imagination he has, the listener will decide that the game is not worth playing, that he is not going to be able to make *any* predictions right, and also stops listening. Too much difference is sameness: boring. Too much sameness is boring—but also different once in a while.[4]

TECHNIQUE VS. EXPRESSIVENESS

A musician cannot express himself or herself in music without sufficient mastery of technique. That is, the musician must possess the instrumental facility to play the musical ideas created in the mind. But technique alone without the element of self-expression is mechanistic and wooden. This is particularly true of the jazz improviser, whose effectiveness is measured by both technique and expressiveness.

Figure 9.9 represents an unbalanced condition in the case of a hypothetical musician who has great desire to express himself but lacks the technique to do so. He is perhaps a three-chord guitarist who has limited proficiency. He has no melody-making skills, no knowledge of keys, of styles, of scales, of standard tunes. In his frustration he resorts to volume, wa-wa, fuzz, and other electronic substitutes for technique. The expressive desire is present but the ability to express is thwarted because of the missing technique.

FIGURE 9.9.

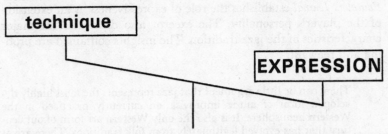

Figure 9.10 represents an unbalanced condition in the case of a hypothetical musician who commands much technique but cannot manage to express himself or to speak to his listeners. He may be a Mr. Super Scales who loads his solos with every imaginable scale, pattern, arpeggiated chord, and well-known cliché, all at top speed, but whose solos lack coherence and expressiveness. This sort of player can also become frustrated because of his inability to communicate something to his listeners. He may add more exotic techniques to his repertoire in the form of circular breathing or altissimo tones, but his problem remains unsolved.

FIGURE 9.10.

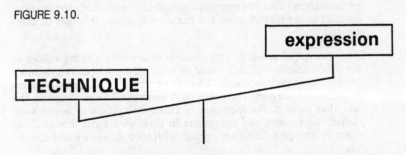

A balance is necessary. The jazz improviser must have valid musical ideas and must possess the technical ability to express those ideas. Most jazz stars have this balance (see figure 9.11).

FIGURE 9.11.

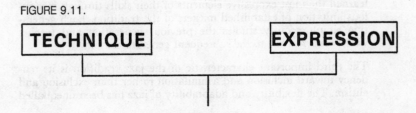

The following excerpt from an article by Bill Dobbins in *Music Educators Journal* establishes the role of expressiveness as an extension of the player's personality. The excerpt also delineates the major characteristics of the jazz tradition. The insights contained are probing and relevant:

There can be little argument that jazz represents the most highly developed form of music improvisation currently practiced in the Western hemisphere. It is also the only Western art form of our century that has evolved legitimately from folk traditions. There are at least four basic concepts integral to the evolution of jazz in America that amply justify this high valuation.

The first and most important concept is that of instrumental sound as an expressive extension of the musician's personality. The actual notes in jazz are often of far less significance than the manner in which they are played. In addition to the usual development of thematic material, a jazz musician attempts to directly express human experience through sound in an intuitive manner beyond the scope of verbal language. The usual comments from listeners following a particularly moving improvisation—such as "He was really saying something" or "He was really telling the truth"—are more revealing, perhaps, than we may suspect. An elusive "something," an unspeakable "truth," is momentarily captured in the greatest jazz performances. This phenomenon completely transcends the particular tune being played as well as the style in which it might be categorized.

The concept of music as an extension of a person's being relates to the jazz musician's unification of all creative musical activities into a whole, integrated approach. Virtually every jazz musician is an interpreter, improviser, composer, and arranger. It was precisely the fact that most of the members of Duke Ellington's orchestra were skilled improvisers and composers in their own right that enabled them to interpret Ellington's music with such authority and conviction.

The second important concept that has been indispensable to the evolution of jazz is its reliance on aural transmission of musical information. Imagine the absurdity of attempting to learn the style of Louis Armstrong from a printed page. Jazz musicians always have learned the most expressive elements of their skills through meticulous imitation of established masters of the tradition. Each generation simultaneously studies the previous generation and teaches what it has learned to the subsequent generation.

The third important characteristic of the jazz tradition is its tendency toward inclusion and assimilation rather than exclusion and elitism. The flexibility and adaptability of jazz has been unequalled in Western music history. Since its initial development by black Americans, jazz has readily assimilated elements from such diverse traditions as European impressionism; Indian, Latin American, and African musics; and numerous American commercial styles. Yet in every new hybrid form the unmistakable expressive qualities rooted in the folk origins of the earliest jazz and blues are immediately recognized by audiences throughout the world. No other form of Western music has proved to be so resilient. It is possible to play a wider range of styles under the guise of being a jazz musician than within the confines of any other contemporary musical category.

The fourth basic concept embodied in the jazz tradition is that of rhythm as a physical rather than an abstract element. Twentieth-century classical composers have tended to treat rhythm as an extremely cerebral element, sometimes controlled by arbitrarily chosen mathematical or serial procedures and sometimes left entirely to chance. Most commercial or pop styles treat rhythm as a totally mechanical element that seldom varies in either pattern or tempo from one work to the next. In the best jazz, however, rhythm is an accurate reflection of the human physical experience: loosely flowing and regularly pulsating at the same time. Jazz frequently superimposes a wide variety of meters over an underlying $\frac{4}{4}$ meter. In this respect jazz has developed the most highly inventive use of common meter in recent Western music.[5]

THE INEQUALITY OF TALENT

The cellist practices orchestral literature, the soprano practices operatic literature, and the jazz instrumentalist practices improvisation. The jazz player spends hours daily practicing scales, patterns, melodic ideas, and tunes, modifying and altering them, all the while steadily branching out from what has already been mastered to something a bit different. This practice engenders growth and the addition of new elements to his or her playing.

Talent, however, is not equal, and some players can consolidate it all and produce a more creative solo than others can. It is not just a matter of experience, although playing experience is certainly important. Nor is it merely a matter of hours of practice, although practice is obviously important. There is also that elusive element known as talent, which some possess to a lesser degree and others to a greater degree. There is no known way to bestow talent, package and disseminate talent, or teach talent. Some musicians display more natural ability for jazz improvisation than others and the result is a marvelous artistry. These are the virtuoso improvisers.

THE ROLE OF THE CRITIC/REVIEWER

When one does not have enough knowledge or experience to feel comfortable in making a personal evaluation of a performance, one may turn to the professional critic for assistance. But how is the critic evaluated? Who reviews the reviewer? Often, an ecstatic blurb on an album cover is giddy, unproductive, and recognizable as such. Observe the following remarks from an album cover:

> *Syeeda* is given a bigger feeling here, with Archie's impeccable arranging of the head, and the head functions here the way any written music ought to, to set the mood, the initial mode, of engagement (attack). Music, otherwise, should be arbitrary (as anything else), i.e., it should reflect only its player (maker). *Syeeda's* head (Trane's "tune") proposes one direction, more or less specific: it produces an image, feeling, sense function . . . extending . . . to where?[6]

What is the reviewer trying to say, exactly? The author of this commentary is passionate about the music, to be sure, but passion is not enough. Usable information is crucial. He says little or nothing about the music or the performance. Only his feelings are described. This is not criticism. In order to judge the performance, usable information is required regarding the musical structures and elements of the performance, not someone's feelings.

Sometimes, however, a scholarly sounding gentleman of the press may cause confusion. His personal prejudices may be cleverly concealed as he tells the reader only what he wishes the reader to hear. In order to evaluate this critic, one must inquire: Is he knowledgeable? Does he know jazz players? Does he know jazz styles? Does he know jazz history? Does he know jazz forms and structures? If the critic does know these things, they will be apparent in his discussion. If the critic does not know these things, little will be learned from his discussion except his enthusiasm or antipathy.

The role of the critic/reviewer should be as follows:

1. To know the subject and the material. If the reviewer is going to pronounce judgments on jazz, then he or she should have expertise in jazz and jazz materials.
2. To knowledgeably describe what occurs. From a description of what takes place *musically,* the reader can get an idea of the performance. Descriptions of subjective feelings impart no hard information at all.

3. To compare with similar performances. A good way to inform the reader about the performance in a general way is to compare the performance to another by the same players or by similar players.

4. To relate new techniques or approaches to existing techniques. By relating the performance to ideas with which the reader is already familiar, the critic imparts information that is useful and clarifying.

5. To give a qualitative assessment based on knowledge and experience. If, for example, the reviewer concludes that the performance is a poor one and if the conclusion is reinforced by his or her command of the subject matter, then the view is at least a reasonable one which may be given serious consideration.

If these characteristics seem to be present in a critic's appraisal of a performance, the reader can then read what he or she has to say with some degree of confidence and respect.

THE IMPORTANCE OF THE COMBO SETTING

Earlier in the discussion of swing, there was a great deal of attention paid to large jazz ensembles, usually called big bands. The swing era existed because of big bands, and the American public for several decades used such bands for social dancing and for entertainment. A well-organized swing band or dance band offered not only dance music for the evening but also a "boy singer," a "girl singer," a vocal group, a comedian (often one of the musicians), novelty numbers, dance contests, and almost anything else they could think of to entertain for three or four hours. These bands offered steady employment for jazz players, although they were infrequently called upon to exhibit more than a hint of their jazz skills in such commercial situations. The bands' main function was to furnish danceable music and musical entertainment.

The combo offered the most congenial surroundings for the jazz player to display improvisational abilities, and although the stage band receives much attention today, the combo setting is still the best one in which to hear a jazz artist perform. In the big band arrangements may often place rigid restraints on the improviser. In the combo setting it is possible for the performance to be more flexible and spontaneous. In the big band there are players who play their written parts very well but who cannot improvise to any great extent and are seldom asked to do so. In the combo all of the players may be improvisers and each one can be called upon to solo. Remarkable innovators such as Charlie Parker, Dizzy Gillespie, John Coltrane, Miles Davis, Elvin Jones, Thelonious Monk, and Art Blakey, just to name a few, are renowned for their work within combos. The combo—the small jazz band made up of from three to eight players—usually offers the listener the best opportunity to hear improvisation at its finest.

In summary, evaluating the jazz improviser requires a familiarity with the historical development of improvisation and an understanding of the similarities between composer and improviser. One should also be aware of the importance of melodic invention in the jazz scheme and know how outside influences affect a performance. One must recognize the necessity for a balance between technique and expressiveness and realize that some performers are more blessed than others with innate jazz abilities. One should learn to assess a jazz review by taking into consideration the reviewer's qualifications and expertise. Finally, one should become familiar with the combo setting as the most appropriate way to display jazz improvisation at its best.

For Suggested Records, Suggestions for Listening, and Suggested Further Readings, see chapter ten.

DEFINING JAZZ

At the end of this study it would be appropriate to try to formulate a workable definition for jazz. How can this remarkable music be defined? Is "Rhapsody in Blue," composed by George Gershwin for symphony orchestra, jazz? Is "Summertime" by George Gershwin, as performed by Lawrence Welk, jazz? Is "Summertime," as played by a marching band for a half-time show, jazz? Is "Summertime," as performed by the Stan Getz Quartet, jazz? Is a John Coltrane treatment of "Summertime" jazz? Is a Sarah Vaughan treatment of "Summertime" jazz?

Where does one start? It is known that jazz is primarily (though not exclusively) an instrumental music and that American popular music is used as a broad basis for concept and style. Jazz is American music by birth but has been adopted by musicians in almost every part of our world and, for the most part, it is an urban music. Jazz cannot be defined without including the word "improvisation." The history of jazz may be outlined by tracing innovators and performers. Invention, modification, and change are essential to maintaining the vitality of this music. Art is not eternal; it must be renewed by each successive generation.

A general definition might be too broad to provide a comfortable grip on the subject, or a precise definition might omit some important elements. Perhaps the following will serve as a starting point:

> Jazz is virtuosic instrumental improvisation and collective creativity, performed within the context of the American popular music idiom.

This definition contains the critical ingredients. It states that jazz is instrumental music, that it incorporates improvisers of virtuosic caliber, that these improvisers react and interact in musically creative ways when placed together in a performing group, and that the source material for this music is or is derived from the American popular idiom.

Not included is the church organist who improvises an interlude for the Sunday service, or the instrumentalist who improvises outside the American popular idiom in an avant-garde music ensemble. Neither the jazz singer nor the jazz dancer is specifically included. It is understood that solitary jazz improvisers such as Oscar Peterson (piano), John Klemmer (tenor sax), or Gary Burton (vibes) are not excluded.

In attempting to define jazz, it should be remembered that in order for such a definition to be valid it must include the ideas of the American popular music idiom, instrumental improvisation, and virtuosity. Thus, the definition stated earlier seems to be a workable one:

> Jazz is virtuosic instrumental improvisation and collective creativity, performed within the context of the American popular music idiom.

SUGGESTED RECORDS:

SUN RA AND HIS ARKESTRA, *The Other Side of the Sun.* SER 1003
GARY BURTON, *Times Square.* ECM 1-1111
Kenny Burrell, John Coltrane. Prestige 24059
JOHNNY GRIFFIN, *Return of the Griffin.* Galaxy 5117
BILLY COBHAM, *Crosswinds.* Atlantic SD-7300
ERIC DOLPHY, *At the Five Spot, vol. 1.* Prestige 7611
JACK DEJOHNETTE, *Untitled.* ECM 1074
JAMES MOODY, *Never Again!* Muse 5001
LARRY YOUNG, *Unity.* Blue Note 4221
MILES DAVIS, *Basic Miles.* Columbia C32025
KEITH JARRETT, *Fort Yawuh.* ABC AS-9240
TOM SCOTT, *Tom Cat.* Ode 77021

SUGGESTIONS FOR LISTENING:

1. Which recordings are mainstream jazz?
2. Which recordings are advanced? Can you determine why?

3. Which recordings contain a high emotive level?
4. Which recordings illustrate a crossover between divergent styles?
5. Do any of the soloists use unusual or specialized instrumental techniques?
6. Do any of the ensembles utilize uncommon instrumental combinations?
7. With regard to listeners' expectations, how does a particular soloist surprise you? How does one bore you? How does one frustrate your expectations? Satisfy your expectations?

SUGGESTED FURTHER READINGS:

Improvising Jazz, Jerry Coker.
Basic Jazz Improvisation, Joseph Levey.
The Jazz Idiom, Jerry Coker; chapter 4.
Understanding Jazz, Leroy Ostransky; chapter 3.
Jazz Styles, Mark C. Gridley; chapter 3.
The Story of Jazz, Marshall W. Stearns; chapter 22.

SELECTED LISTENING NOTES

CHAPTER ONE

Clark Terry, *Big B-A-D Band Live*

Side 1:

BAND 1 "Una Mas"
Solos: Arnie Lawrence, alto sax; Jimmy Wilkins, trombone; Clark Terry, trumpet; Charles Davis, baritone sax; Ed Soph, drums.

BAND 4 "Randi"
Slow ballad playing. Solo: Phil Woods, alto sax.

Side 2:

BAND 2 "Sheba"
Solos: Clark Terry, trumpet (from slow to double time); Ernie Wilkins, tenor sax.

BAND 3 "Cold Tater Stomp"
Good example of 12-bar blues for big band. Solos: Clark Terry, muted trumpet; Janice Robinson, trombone.

Akiyoshi/Tabackin, *Long Yellow Road*

Side A:

BAND 1 "Long Yellow Road"
Solos: Gary Foster, alto sax; Don Rader, trumpet.

119

BAND 2 "The First Night"
Blues-influenced harmony. Solo: Bobby Shew, flugel-horn.

BAND 3 "Opus Number Zero"
Solos: Chuck Flores, drums; Don Rader, trumpet; Gene Cherico, bass (walking style); Charlie Loper, trombone; Toshiko Akiyoshi, piano; Dick Spencer, alto sax; Lew Tabackin, tenor sax.

Side B:

BAND 1 "Quadrille, Anyone?"
Blues-influenced composition. Solos: Bill Perkins, bari-tone sax; Gary Foster, soprano sax; Lew Tabackin, tenor sax.

Thad Jones/Mel Lewis, *Consummation*

Side 1:

BAND 1 "Dedication"
Solo: Jerome Richardson, alto sax.

BAND 3 "Tiptoe"
Staccato sax section writing is featured. Solos: Snooky Young, trumpet; Mel Lewis, drums (brushes); Jerry Dodgion, alto sax.

Side 2:

BAND 1 "Ahunk Ahunk"
$\frac{5}{4}$-meter blues. Solos: Roland Hanna, electronic piano; Eddie Daniels, tenor sax; Marvin Stamm, trumpet.

BAND 2 "Fingers"
Fast 32-bar tune. Solos: Benny Powell, trombone; Danny Moore, muted trumpet; Billy Harper, tenor sax; Roland Hanna, piano; Richard Davis, walking bass.

Heath Brothers, *Passing Through*

Side 1:

BAND 1 "A New Blue"
Modified 12-bar blues. Solos: Tony Purrone, guitar; Jimmy Heath, tenor sax.

BAND 2 "In New York"
Chord changes to "Body and Soul." Solos: Percy Heath, bass; Stanley Cowell, piano; Jimmy Heath, tenor sax.

Side 2:

BAND 1 "Mellowdrama"
Pop style. Solos: Jimmy Heath, soprano sax; Tony Purrone, guitar.

BAND 4 "Prince Albert"
Chord changes to "All the Things You Are." Theme: tenor sax & guitar in unison. Solos: Stanley Cowell, piano; Jimmy Heath, tenor sax; Percy Heath, bass.

Oscar Peterson, *The Oscar Peterson Big 6 at the Montreux Jazz Festival, 1975*

Side 1:

BAND 1 "Au Privave"
12-bar blues. Solos: Toots Thielemans, harmonica; Joe Pass, guitar; Milt Jackson, vibes; Oscar Peterson, piano; Niels Pedersen, bass.

BAND 2 "Here's That Rainy Day"
Slow ballad. Solos by all of the above.

Side 2:

BAND 2 "Reunion Blues"
12-bar blues. Solos by all including Louis Bellson, drums.

Gerry Mulligan, *Gerry Mulligan Quartet*
Gerry Mulligan, baritone sax; Bob Brookmeyer, valve trombone; Red Mitchell, bass; Frank Isola, drums. No piano or comping.

Side A1:

BAND 1 "I May Be Wrong"
Solos: Gerry Mulligan, baritone sax; Bob Brookmeyer, valve trombone.

Side A2:

BAND 1 "Makin' Whoopie"
Notice supporting countermelody helping to fill in the missing comping.

BAND 3 "Love Me or Leave Me"
Same textures as above.

Buddy Rich, *Stick It*
Side 1:

BAND 1 "Space Shuttle"
Fast "straight-ahead" jazz. Solo: Pat LaBarbera, soprano sax.

BAND 3 "Best Coast"
Jazz waltz. Solos: Pat LaBarbera, soprano sax; Eric Culver, trombone.

Side 2:

BAND 3 "Sassy Strut"
Funky composition. Solos: Pat LaBarbera, soprano sax; Walt Namuth, guitar; Joe Romano, alto sax.

The Art of the Modern Jazz Quartet
John Lewis, piano; Milt Jackson, vibes; Percy Heath, bass; Connie Kay, drums.

Side 1:

BAND 3 "Bag's Groove"
12-bar blues. Guest artist: Sonny Rollins, tenor sax.

Side 2:

BAND 1 "The Cylinder"
Modal harmony and 12-bar blues.

Side 3:

BAND 3 "Bluesology"
12-bar blues.

BAND 4 "Spanish Steps"
Minor mode. Impressionistic intro followed by jazz waltz, then fast section.

Irakere, *Irakere*
A contemporary Cuban band.

Side 1:

BAND 1 "Juana Mil Ciento"
A long drums and percussion intro, then a bass ostinato with guitar, then brass and saxes, then singing, then full ensemble. Short tenor sax, trumpet, and guitar solos.

BAND 2 "Ilya"
Similar to jazz-rock fusion. Solos by guitar, trumpet (using altissimo register), tenor sax. Band members are introduced.

Gato Barbieri, *Bolivia*
A contemporary South American group.

Side 1:

BAND 1 "Merceditas"
A composition of several different parts and tempos. Solos: Gato Barbieri, tenor sax; Lonnie Liston Smith, piano.

Side 2:

BAND 2 "Niños"
Intro is a bass ostinato with rhythm section. Solos: Gato Barbieri, tenor sax; Lonnie Liston Smith, piano.

Elvin Jones, *The Main Force*

Side 1:

BAND 1 "Salty Iron"
Solos: Dave Liebman, soprano sax; Ryo Kawasaki, guitar; Al Dailey, keyboard.

Side 2:

BAND 2 "Song of Rejoicing after Returning from a Hunt"
Adapted by Elvin Jones from the Djoboko Rhythm of the Ba-Benzele Pygmies. Note the drum set playing, additional percussion, and clapping. Solos: Frank Foster, tenor sax; Ryo Kawasaki, guitar.

Joanne Brackeen, *Tring-a-Ling*

Side 1:

BAND 1   "Shadowbrook-Aire"
The head followed by solos. Later there are short bursts of solos exchanged between players. Solos: Mike Brecker, tenor sax; Joanne Brackeen, piano; Cecil McBee, bass.

Side 2:

BAND 1   "Haiti-B"
In $\frac{7}{4}$ meter. Solos: Mike Brecker, tenor sax ("outside" style); Joanne Brackeen, piano; Billy Hart, drums.

Gene Ammons, *Got My Own*

Side 1:

BAND 2   "God Bless the Child"
A slow tempo with double-time effect from drums. Solo: Gene Ammons, tenor sax.

Side 2:

BAND 3   "Tin Shack Out Back"
Traditional 12-bar blues. Solos: Maynard Parker, guitar; Gene Ammons, tenor sax; Sonny Phillips, piano.

Art Blakey, *Buhaina*
Art Blakey and the Jazz Messengers

Side 1:

BAND 2   "A Chant for Bu"
Minor mode. Solos: Woody Shaw, trumpet; Carter Jefferson, soprano sax; Michael Howell, guitar; Cedar Walton, piano.

Side 2:

BAND 1   "Mission Eternal"
Samba rhythm. Note Blakey's drums behind solos. Solos: Woody Shaw, trumpet; Carter Jefferson, tenor sax; Michael Howell, guitar; Cedar Walton, piano; Art Blakey, drums.

Freddie Hubbard, *Red Clay*

Side A:

BAND 1 "Red Clay"
A free intro, then into tempo. Head is blues-like. Solos:
Freddie Hubbard, trumpet; Herbie Hancock, keyboard;
Joe Henderson, tenor sax; Ron Carter, bass.

Side B:

BAND 2 "The Intrepid Fox"
A complex head. Solos: Freddie Hubbard, trumpet; Joe
Henderson, tenor sax; Herbie Hancock, piano.

Woody Shaw, *Moontrane*

Side A:

BAND 1 "Moontrane"
A modal-influenced tune. Solos: Woody Shaw, trumpet;
Azar Lawrence, tenor sax; Onaje Allen Gumbs, piano;
Victor Lewis, drums; Buster Williams, bass.

Side B:

BAND 1 "Sanyas"
Free intro with conch shell, continued free intro with
horns. Cecil McBee's bass solo then becomes an ostinato
and horns enter. Latin-style rhythm. Solos: Steve Turre,
trombone; Azar Lawrence, soprano sax; Woody Shaw,
trumpet; Onaje Allen Gumbs, piano; Guilherme Franco,
percussion.

Dizzy Gillespie, *The Dizzy Gillespie Big 7 at the Montreux Jazz Festival,
1975*

Side 2:

BAND 2 "Cherokee"
Fast tempo, 32-bar tune. A jazz favorite for improvising.
Two tenors play the head and Dizzy plays a droll coun-
termelody. Solos: Eddie "Lockjaw" Davis, tenor sax;
Dizzy Gillespie, trumpet; Milt Jackson, vibes; Johnny
Griffin, tenor sax; Mickey Roker, drums. Others trade 4-
bar solos with drums.

African and Afro-American Drums

Side 2:

BAND 6 "Salute to a Chief"
Nigeria, the Yoruba

BAND 7 "Drums for a Deity"
Nigeria, the Yoruba

BAND 8 "Dance Drums"
Belgian Congo, the Bambala
In these selections note the subtle shifting accents over the steady basic pulse.

CHAPTERS FOUR AND FIVE

Miles Davis, *Water Babies*

Side 1:

BAND 2 "Capricorn"
Trumpet solo (Davis) is supported by bass (Ron Carter) and drums (Tony Williams), but no keyboard. Tenor sax solo (Wayne Shorter) is treated in the same manner. Keyboard solo (Herbie Hancock) follows. It is not chordal but almost entirely right-hand melody. Theme ends the presentation.

Side 2:

BAND 1 "Two Faced"
Notice the floating or loose trumpet solo placed against an active rhythm section. Bass converses with keyboard. The two horns play the theme in an echo pattern. Solos: Miles Davis, trumpet; Wayne Shorter, tenor sax; Herbie Hancock, keyboard.

Jack Williams, *Merge*

Side 1:

BAND 1 "Fum"
Head played by trumpet and guitar in unison. The piece is in samba rhythm and the form is AABA. Solos: Randy Brecker, trumpet; Jack Wilkins, guitar; Jack DeJohnette, drums; Eddie Gomez, bass.

BAND 1 "Buds"
A complex head in samba rhythm. Solos: Jack Wilkins, guitar; Randy Brecker, flugelhorn.

BAND 3 "500 Miles High"
A bass and guitar duet (Gomez and Wilkins). Bowed bass is overdubbed with plucked (pizzicato) bass.

Clare Fischer, *Easy Livin'*

Side 2:

BAND 1 "I'll Take Romance"
Solo piano (Fischer) accompanied by bass (Bobby West), done in a jazz waltz style. Notice in the piano solo the continued inventiveness and imagination used on this old standard tune.

Jim Hall/Ron Carter, *Alone Together*

Side 1:

BAND 4 "I'll Remember April"
Guitar and bass duo. Note how Carter's bass style changes from arpeggiated and fragmented to walking style. Guitar comps behind bass solo.

Side 2:

BAND 4 "Autumn Leaves"
Statement-and-answer style (a kind of call and response) between the two instruments. In a later section, more of a swing style.

Hubert Laws, *Carnegie Hall*

Side 1:

"Windows"
This is a Chick Corea composition in $\frac{3}{4}$ meter which enjoys much popularity among jazz musicians. Note the clean, precise flute technique. Solos: Hubert Laws, flute; Dave Friedman, vibes; Bob James, piano.

Cannonball Adderly, *Inside Straight*

Side 1:

BAND 3   "Saudade"
A Latin rhythm. Solos: Cannonball Adderly, alto sax; Nat Adderly, trumpet; Hal Galper, electric piano.

Side 2:

BAND 2   "Five of a Kind"
Minor mode and fast. Note the imaginative support given solos by drums and bass. Solos: Cannonball Adderly, alto sax; Nat Adderly, trumpet; Hal Galper, electric piano; Roy McCurdy, drums.

Brecker Brothers, *Back to Back*

Side 1:

BAND 4   "Night Flight"
High energy jazz-rock fusion in a minor mode. Solos: Randy Brecker, electric trumpet; Mike Brecker, tenor sax; Steve Gadd, drums.

Side 2:

BAND 1   "Slick Stuff"
A complex head using flute for one section. Note how drums reinforce ensemble accents. Solos: Randy Brecker, trumpet; Mike Brecker, tenor sax; Christopher Parker, drums.

Dexter Gordon, *Homecoming*

Side 4:

BAND 1   " 'Round Midnight"
The well-known Thelonious Monk composition played fairly straight at first. Flugelhorn countermelody played by Woody Shaw. Flugelhorn solo is more active than Gordon's smooth, serene approach to the tune. Solos: Dexter Gordon, tenor sax; Woody Shaw, flugelhorn; Ronnie Mathews, piano.

BAND 2   "Backstairs"
Fast 12-bar blues. Rhythm section plays intro. Note the quotes in Gordon's solo. Solos: Dexter Gordon, tenor sax; Woody Shaw, trumpet; Ronnie Mathews, piano.

CHAPTER SIX

Bob Mover, *Bob Mover*

Side 1:

BAND 1 "Sweet Basil"
This tune uses the chord changes from "Cherokee." In the first alto solo chorus, the rhythm section plays in stop time. Solos: Claudio Roditi, trumpet; Bob Mover, alto sax; Kenny Barron, piano; Ben Riley, drums.

BAND 2 "We'll Be Together Again"
Sensitive slow-ballad playing by Mover. Ends with an alto sax cadenza. Solos: Bob Mover, alto sax; Ron McClure, bass.

Side 2:

BAND 3 "Milestones"
Solos: Claudio Roditi, trumpet; Bob Mover, soprano sax; Kenny Barron, piano.

John Coltrane, *The Best of John Coltrane*

Side 1:

BAND 1 "My Favorite Things"
The well-known Rodgers and Hammerstein show song done in a jazz waltz style. An extension of several bars is attached to the end of the original melody. Modal harmony is employed with the Rodgers music. Solos: McCoy Tyner, piano; John Coltrane, soprano sax.

BAND 3 "Giant Steps"
The world-famous Coltrane composition. This tenor sax solo has been imitated, orchestrated, transcribed, and analyzed by scholars. Note the intensity with which it is played and the continued, inspired improvisation. The piano soloist is Tommy Flanagan.

Al Dimeola, *Land of the Midnight Sun*

Side 1:

BAND 1 "The Wizard"
Solos: Al Dimeola, six- and twelve-string-guitars. This piece uses ostinatos and modal harmonies.

    BAND 2 "Short Tales of the Black Forest"
Duet between Chick Corea, piano and marimba, and Dimeola, guitar. The piece is loosely structured and employs collective improvisation.

Thad Jones/Mel Lewis, *The Jazz Orchestra*

Side 1:

    BAND 1 "Once Around"
Notice the different degrees of dynamics and energy used. Solos: Bill Berry, muted trumpet; Pepper Adams, baritone sax; Hank Jones, piano; Mel Lewis, drums.

Side 2:

    BAND 1 "Mean What You Say"
The Hank Jones piano solo is the intro. Trombone section is featured toward the end. Solos: Thad Jones, flugelhorn; Eddie Daniels, tenor sax.

Lee Konitz, *The Lee Konitz Nonet*

Side 1:

    BAND 5 "Giant Steps"
The John Coltrane composition. Alto and baritone saxes play part of the original Coltrane solo in unison. Solos: Ronnie Cuber, baritone sax; Burt Collins, trumpet; Lee Konitz, alto sax; Kenny Washington, drums.

Side 2:

    BAND 1 "April/April Too"
Uses the chord changes from "I'll Remember April." Ends with a bop-style head which matches "April" chord changes. Solos: Ben Aranov, piano; Lee Konitz, alto sax; Jim Knepper, trombone; John Eckert, flugelhorn; Ronnie Cuber, baritone sax.

Horace Silver, *In Pursuit of the 27th Man*

Side 1:

    BAND 1 "Liberated Brother"
Typical of Silver's compositional style. Solos: Randy Brecker, trumpet; Mike Brecker, tenor sax; Horace Silver, piano.

BAND 1 "Nothin' Can Stop Me"
Funky treatment of a jazz waltz. Chord progression is blues-derived. Note call-and-response effect between ensemble and Silver's solo piano.

Sonny Stitt, *Constellation*

Side A:

BAND 1 "Constellation"
A Charlie Parker composition based on "I Got Rhythm" 32-bar chord progression. Solos: Sonny Stitt, alto sax; Barry Harris, piano.

BAND 2 "Ghost of a Chance"
Slow ballad style. Ends with a free cadenza. Solo: Sonny Stitt, tenor sax.

Side B:

BAND 1 "Ray's Idea"
A bop standard tune. A relaxed tempo. Solos: Sonny Stitt, alto sax; Barry Harris, piano.

Gary Burton/Chick Corea, *Crystal Silence*

Side 1:

BAND 1 "Señor Mouse"
An interesting Corea composition in a quasi-Spanish style. Burton's vibes technique is apparent here. Vibes play a soft ostinato as piano takes foreground.

Side 2:

BAND 2 "Falling Grace"
Jazz feel without obvious rhythm clichés. A lively duet texture.

CHAPTER SEVEN

Phil Woods, *Musique du Bois*

Side A:

BAND 1 "Samba du Bois"
Note the quiet beginning and the gradual increase in

energy and intensity. Solos: Phil Woods, alto sax; Jaki Byard, piano.

Side B:

BAND 3 "Airegin"
The Sonny Rollins composition ("Nigeria" spelled backwards). Note the continued melodic ingenuity applied to the tune by Woods. Solos: Phil Woods, alto sax; Jaki Byard, piano; Richard Davis, bass (rapid walking style); Alan Dawson, drums.

Sonny Fortune, *Awakening*

Side 1:

BAND 1 "Triple Threat"
Note the different approaches to improvising on the same tune as presented by the several soloists. Solos: Sonny Fortune, alto sax; Charles Sullivan, trumpet; Kenny Barron, piano; Wayne Dockery, bass.

BAND 2 "Nommo"
A modal-type piece with a funky quality. Solos: Reggie Workman, bass; Kenny Barron, piano; Sonny Fortune, alto sax.

Richie Cole, *Hollywood Madness*

Side A:

BAND 1 "Hooray for Hollywood"
The old tune of yesteryear played at break-neck speed. Solos: Richie Cole, alto sax; Dick Hindman, piano; Les DeMerle, drums.

BAND 2 "Hi-Fly"
Samba-style. Solos: Richie Cole, alto sax; Bruce Forman, guitar; Dick Hindman, piano; Eddie Jefferson, scat vocal.

Don Cherry, *The Avant-Garde*

Side 2:

BAND 2 "The Invisible"
Note that there is no comping instrument used. Solos:

Don Cherry, trumpet; John Coltrane, tenor sax; Ed Blackwell, drums.

BAND 3 "Bemsha Swing"
Tune composed by Thelonious Monk. Note the trumpet phrasing and tone quality. Solos: Don Cherry, trumpet; John Coltrane, tenor sax; Percy Heath, bass; Ed Blackwell, drums.

Ted Curson, *Jubilant Power*

Side A:

BAND 1 "Reava's Waltz"
12-bar blues in a fast $\frac{3}{4}$ meter. Note the background riffs behind the solos. With the alto solo, the texture at one point diminishes to alto and bass. Solos: Ted Curson, trumpet; Nick Brignola, baritone sax; Chris Woods, alto sax; Andy LaVerne, piano; David Friesen, bass.

BAND 2 "Ted's Tempo"
Fast minor-mode 32-bar tune. Bass ostinato helps outline tune. Solos are traded around at the end. Solos: Ted Curson, flugelhorn; Nick Brignola, baritone sax; Chris Woods, alto sax; Andy LaVerne, piano.

Chet Baker, *You Can't Go Home Again*

Side 1:

BAND 1 "Love for Sale"
The well-known Cole Porter tune in a fresh jazz-rock style. Solos: Michael Brecker, tenor sax; Chet Baker, trumpet; John Scofield, electric guitar; Alphonso Johnson, electric bass; Ron Carter, acoustic bass.

BAND 2 "Un Poco Loco"
Solos: John Scofield, electric guitar; Michael Brecker, tenor sax; Chet Baker, trumpet; Tony Williams, drums.

John Coltrane, *Blue Train*

Side 1:

BAND 2 "Moment's Notice"
The popular Coltrane composition here performed by the originator. Each chorus contains a solo break to send

the soloist into the next repetition. Solos: John Coltrane, tenor sax; Curtis Fuller, trombone; Lee Morgan, trumpet; Paul Chambers, bowed bass; Kenny Drew, piano.

Side 2:

BAND 1 "Locomotion"
Fast-tempo 12-bar blues with an 8-bar extension. Ending contains a tenor solo. Solos: John Coltrane, tenor sax; Curtis Fuller, trombone; Lee Morgan, trumpet; Kenny Drew, piano; "Philly" Joe Jones, drums.

CHAPTER EIGHT

From *The Smithsonian Collection of Classic Jazz*, solos by the following artists:

Louis Armstrong, trumpet:
Side 2:

BAND 5 "Struttin' with Some Barbeque"
Side 2:

BAND 6 "S.O.L. Blues"
Side 2:

BAND 7 "Potato Head Blues"

Dizzy Gillespie, trumpet:
Side 7:

BAND 6 "Shaw 'Nuff"

Miles Davis, trumpet:
Side 11:

BAND 3 "So What"

J. J. Johnson, trombone:
Side 8:

BAND 2 "Little Benny"

Johnny Hodges, alto sax:
Side 7:
> BAND 1   "In a Mellotone"

Charlie Parker, alto sax:
Side 7:
> BAND 6   "Shaw 'Nuff"
Side 7:
> BAND 7   "Ko Ko"

Sidney Bechet, clarinet:
Side 2:
> BAND 3   "Blue Horizon"

Coleman Hawkins, tenor sax:
Side 4:
> BAND 4   "Body and Soul"

Lester Young, tenor sax:
Side 5:
> BAND 7   "Doggin' Around"
Side 6:
> BAND 1   "Lester Leaps In"

Benny Goodman, clarinet:
Side 6:
> BAND 2   "I Found a New Baby"

James P. Johnson, piano:
Side 2:
> BAND 4   "Carolina Shout"

Art Tatum, piano:

Side 5:

    BAND 1   "Willow Weep for Me"

Side 5:

    BAND 2   "Too Marvelous for Words"

Bud Powell, piano:

Side 8:

    BAND 5   "Somebody Loves Me"

Thelonious Monk, piano:

Side 9:

    BAND 4   "Misterioso"

Side 9:

    BAND 7   "Smoke Gets in Your Eyes"

Jimmy Blanton, bass:

Side 7:

    BAND 2   "Ko Ko"

Elvin Jones, drums:

Side 12:

    BAND 4   "Alabama"

Charlie Christian, guitar:

Side 6:

    BAND 2   "I Found a New Baby"

Side 6:

    BAND 3   "Blues Sequence"

Lionel Hampton, vibraphone:

Side 5:

    BAND 6   "When Lights Are Low"

Don Ellis, *Electric Bath*

Side 1:

BAND 1 "Indian Lady"
Funky composition in $\frac{5}{4}$.

Side 1:

BAND 3 "Turkish Bath"
12-bar blues in $\frac{7}{4}$ with quarter-tone effect in the reed section. Solos: Don Ellis, trumpet; Ron Meyers, trombone; Joe Roccisano, soprano sax; Mike Lang, clarinet.

CHAPTERS NINE AND TEN

Sun Ra and his Arkestra, *The Other Side of the Sun*

Side 1:

BAND 3 "Space Is the Place"
Intro uses electronics and spacey instrumental sounds. Solo singer, random singers, and random instrumental solos. In spite of some radical elements, the piece uses normal time and chord progressions.

Side 2:

BAND 3 "Manhattan Cocktail"
Collective improvisation in a free setting with no time frame. Different energy levels and textures are created.

Gary Burton, *Times Square*

Side 1:

BAND 1 "Semblance"
The vibes comp behind the trumpet solo. Solos: Gary Burton, vibes; Tiger Okoshi, muted trumpet; Roy Haynes, drums.

Side 2:

BAND 2 "Radio"
An interesting chord progression. Active drums beneath solos. Solos: Gary Burton, vibes; Steve Swallow, bass.

BAND 3 "True or False"
A free drum set solo by Roy Haynes.

Kenny Burrell, John Coltrane

Side 2:

BAND 1 "Freight Trane"
12-bar blues format. At the end, 4-bar phrases are traded between tenor sax and guitar. Solos: John Coltrane, tenor sax; Kenny Burrell, guitar; Tommy Flanagan, piano; Paul Chambers, bowed bass.

Side 3:

BAND 1 "Minor Mishap"
A 32-bar tune in a minor mode, with 4-bar phrases traded with Louis Hayes, drums. Solos: John Coltrane, tenor sax; Kenny Burrell, guitar; Idrees Sulieman, trumpet; Tommy Flanagan, piano.

Johnny Griffin, Return of the Griffin

Side 1:

BAND 1 "Autumn Leaves"
Multiple choruses by a virtuoso improviser. Solos: Johnny Griffin, tenor sax; Ronnie Mathews, piano; Keith Copeland, drums.

BAND 2 "A Monk's Dream"
A composition in the style of Thelonious Monk. Pianist adopts some of Monk's mannerisms. Solos: Johnny Griffin, tenor sax; Ronnie Mathews, piano; Ray Drummond, bass.

Billy Cobham, Crosswinds

Side 1:

BAND 4 "Flash Flood"
Fusion or jazz-rock with high-energy drumming by Cobham. Solos: Randy Brecker, electric trumpet; John Abercrombie, electric guitar.

Side 2:

BAND 1 "The Pleasant Pheasant"
Solos: Michael Brecker, tenor sax; George Duke, synthesizer; Billy Cobham, drums.

Eric Dolphy, *At the Five Spot, vol. 1*

Side A:

BAND 1   "Fire Waltz"

A simple tune in waltz time style which allows the soloist room to stretch out. Solos: Eric Dolphy, alto sax; Booker Little, trumpet (he quotes "How High the Moon"); Mal Waldron, piano.

BAND 2   "Bee Vamp"

Solos: Booker Little, trumpet; Eric Dolphy, bass clarinet (great artistry on this unlikely jazz instrument); Mal Waldron, piano; Richard Davis, bass.

Jack DeJohnette, *Untitled*

Side 1:

BAND 1   "Flying Spirits"

Sensitive exchange of ideas and use of collective improvisation. Solos: Jack DeJohnnette, drums; Alex Foster, soprano sax; John Abercrombie, electric guitar; Warren Bernhardt, electric piano.

James Moody, *Never Again!*

Side B:

BAND 1   "St. Thomas"

The calypso tune written by Sonny Rollins. Outstanding bop tenor playing. Solos: James Moody, tenor sax; Mickey Tucker, organ; Eddie Gladden, drums.

BAND 3   "Freedom Jazz Dance"

This more radical form requires a more radical playing style. Solos: James Moody, tenor sax; Mickey Tucker, organ; Roland Wilson, electric bass.

Larry Young, *Unity*

Side 1:

BAND 1   "Zoltan"

Essentially a two-chord harmonic progression. Notice the drums accompaniment for the solos. Solos: Woody

Shaw, trumpet; Joe Henderson, tenor sax; Larry Young, organ; Elvin Jones, drums.

BAND 3 "If"
A blues-like tune. Note that Young is his own bassist using the bass register of the organ. Solos: Joe Henderson, tenor sax; Woody Shaw, trumpet; Larry Young, organ.

Miles Davis, *Basic Miles*

Side 2:

BAND 1 "On Green Dolphin Street"
A jazz standard. Note the locked hands piano style. Solos: Bill Evans, piano intro; Miles Davis, muted trumpet; John Coltrane, tenor sax; Cannonball Adderly, alto sax; Bill Evans, piano.

BAND 3 "Fran-Dance"
Solos: Cannonball Adderly, alto sax; John Coltrane, tenor sax; Wynton Kelly, piano.

Keith Jarrett, *Fort Yawuh*

Side 1:

BAND 1 "(If the) Misfits (Wear It)"
Note the high-energy rhythm section without a defined time pulse and the singing through the tenor sax. Solos: Keith Jarrett, piano; Dewey Redman, tenor sax; Paul Motian, drums.

Side 2:

BAND 1 "De Drums"
Heavy use of ostinato in a funky context. Solos: Keith Jarrett, piano; Dewey Redman, tenor sax.

Tom Scott, *Tom Cat*

Side 1:

BAND 1 "Rock Island Rocket"
A modulating blues composition. Note the use of the altissimo register on tenor sax. Solos: Larry Nash, elec-

tronic piano; Robben Ford, electric guitar; Tom Scott, tenor sax.

Side 2:

BAND 1 "Good Evening Mr. and Mrs. America and All the Ships at Sea"
High-energy jazz-rock fusion. Solos: Robben Ford, electric guitar; Tom Scott, tenor sax.

ABOUT RECORDINGS

There are jazz fans whose primary interest in jazz is the collection of recordings. They specialize in acquiring recordings of certain players, certain historical periods, or particular performances. Then there are jazz devotees who believe that live performances are the only way to listen to jazz. In reality, there is much to be said for both kinds of listening.

Certainly, recordings are instructional, and a serious student may analyze a performance measure by measure and note by note through the repeated playing of a recording. The student may also trace the gradual development of a particular player's style through a chronological study of records made by the performer. These processes are particularly valuable for the historian or the aspiring instrumentalist who wishes to study jazz performance techniques.

Recorded jazz improvisations are initially extemporaneous instrumental utterances; they are improvised totalities, produced spontaneously and subsequently frozen in time through the recording process. To hear a live jazz performance, however, realizing that it is a newly conceived version of the piece being improvised, that it has never been interpreted exactly as it is now being heard, and that it will never again be performed in exactly the same way, is truly exciting. And, of course, if this vivid performance is being recorded to preserve the moment forever, then it is possible to relive and reexperience the excitement.

Whichever method a jazz listener may prefer, recordings of jazz have existed almost from the beginnings of the history of jazz to the present, and recorded jazz has become an indispensable part of the jazz spectrum.

The recordings suggested in this book are an eclectic selection demonstrating the variety and choice available to the listener. They are, however, only a fraction of what may be obtained, and the compilation of an extensive, usable discography presents certain difficulties. It is nearly impossible to produce a discography that may be used intact for any reasonable length of time, because recordings are in a perpetual state of flux; records are discontinued, reissued, or placed in new collections, and record companies are regularly going out of business or being swallowed up by corporate conglomerates. The jazz recording business shows no signs of altering this state of impermanence, but the following books may be helpful in assembling a discography for your own personal use.

> *Jazz: A History,* by Frank Tirro, contains a comprehensive list of discographies under the Bibliography section. There is also a Selected Discography.
>
> *Jazz City,* by Leroy Ostransky, contains a detailed Selective Discography organized around the historically important jazz cities. Background recordings are included.
>
> *Jazz Styles,* by Mark C. Gridley, contains an informative chapter (20) entitled "Guide to Record Buying," a list of rare record dealers (table 20.2), and a very detailed Discography section.
>
> *Listening to Jazz,* by Jerry Coker, contains an excellent list of Dealers in Discontinued Records and Tapes. It also contains an admirable chapter ("The Improviser's Hall of Fame") which, although heavily emphasizing saxophonists, carries a good discography for each artist discussed.

GLOSSARY

ARPEGGIATED CHORD. A chord played so that the individual notes are sounded one at a time instead of being sounded simultaneously. Often played in order from the lowest to the highest.

ARRANGEMENT. An orchestrated version of an existing composition.

ARTICULATION. Common in wind instrument notation and indicated by symbols placed over notes to signify the manner of attacking and releasing individual tones. Also see *legato tonguing* and *hard tonguing*.

BLOCK CHORD. A chord of four or more notes, usually constructed in a symmetrical pattern of scale intervals (thirds).

BLUES FORM. A set of chords placed in twelve measures of musical time. This twelve-measure length and each of the individual chords are subject to considerable modification by performers without damaging the blues quality and character.

BLUES PROGRESSION. The characteristic chordal relationships at key locations in the blues form.

BLUES SCALE. A series of tones in a scale-like pattern that imparts the blues quality and character in melodic terms without chords of accompaniment.

BOOGIE WOOGIE. A piano style most often based on blues chord changes. The characteristic feature is the repetitive left-hand rhythm of eight notes per measure.

BOP. (re-bop, be-bop) A style of performing, improvising, and composing, ca. 1940–1955.

BRIDGE. The name given to the B section of the A A B A form, thirty-two measure song. It is eight measures in length, and connects the initial A material with a final statement of A material.

CADENZA. A virtuosic solo, usually unaccompanied and in free time, often located at the end of a tune.

CALL AND RESPONSE. A type of group singing or playing involving a leader (the call) and an answering group (the response).

CHART. Another name for a written arrangement or a composition. *See also* Arrangement.

CHORD. A group of three or more tones, sounded simultaneously, which is an identifiable unit to the ear.

CHORD PROGRESSION. A series of chords, each of which progresses to the next with some sort of musical logic toward a conclusive tonal goal.

CLICHÉ. A musical idea or motive which is made commonplace through overuse.

COLLECTIVE IMPROVISATION. A characteristic of Dixieland jazz denoting several individual instrumentalists improvising solos simultaneously. Has also become a part of some types of modern free jazz.

COMBO. A small jazz ensemble, often three, four, or five instrumentalists.

COMPING. Accompanimental chording, usually performed on a chording instrument such as piano, guitar, organ, accordion, or vibes. Used to support an improvised solo and usually performed in syncopated rhythms.

COUNTERMELODY. A complementary melody performed simultaneously with the original melody. A simple counterpoint that may be improvised or composed.

DOUBLE. Additional instruments on which a jazz player will perform.

DRUM SET. The collection of drums and cymbals on which the jazz drummer performs. Commonly a bass drum with foot pedal, a snare drum, one or more tom-toms, a hi-hat cymbal with foot pedal, a ride cymbal, and a crash cymbal.

ENSEMBLE. A performing group, a group of instrumentalists.

FEED-IN. A drummer's fill, specifically one that announces a forthcoming solo or a forthcoming ensemble phrase.

FILLS. The insertion of additional musical material in an empty space between the end of one phrase and the beginning of the next phrase. Most often a function of the drummer, although fills may be played by any instrument.

FORM. The outer shape of a piece of music, determined by the sequence of musical events that have occurred.

FUNKY. Music that is unrefined, emotive, earthy, or gospel-like in character.

FUSION. A crossover or combining of some elements from two distinct musical styles. An example might be elements from hard bop combined with elements from rock to form jazz-rock.

GLISS. (glissando) Sliding smoothly from one pitch to another so that one hears only an even glide to a higher or lower pitch level.

HARD TONGUING. A hard attack (like saying "TU") to initiate a tone on a wind instrument.

HARMONY. Chordal support that enhances and complements melody. Also see *chord* and *chord progression*.

HEAD. The tune or theme of any jazz composition. The original melody as invented by its composer.

IMPROVISATION. The most important factor in jazz playing, the ability to solo with a tune, performing it with freedom and spontaneity and reinterpreting it in a creative manner.

INSTRUMENTATION. The instruments used or called for in a particular musical presentation.

KEY. A tonal center or home base tone for a piece or a section of a piece of music. The melody and harmony gravitate toward and around this keynote and use it or imply it in their structures.

LEAD SHEET. The publisher's original version of a song, comprised of the original melody, chord symbols, and lyrics.

LEGATO TONGUING. A soft attack (like saying "DU") for a tone on a wind instrument.

LICKS. Melodic or rhythmic ideas, borrowed or newly invented.

LOCKED HANDS. A piano style that creates a smoother effect than ragtime or stride. It involves moving both hands in the same direction to create a flowing chordal texture.

MAINSTREAM. A word used to describe middle-of-the-road music, that which is neither too radical nor too conservative.

METER. Regular, recurring accent in music. For example í 2 ȝ́ 4, í 2 ȝ́ 4, or í 2 3, í 2 3, etc. Designated in notation by meter signs such as $\frac{4}{4}$, $\frac{2}{4}$, or $\frac{3}{4}$, etc.

MODES. Scales once popular among medieval and renaissance musicians, they began to be used again as improvisational materials by jazz players in the 1960s and 1970s. They have a fresh or folk-like quality and jazz players favor the Dorian mode for a minor flavor and the Mixolydian mode for a major flavor. Jazz musicians also use the term "modal" for music with minimal chord change activity (only one or two chords).

MODULATE. The transference of emphasis from one tonal center to a second tonal center. Also see *key*.

MUTE. A device placed in the bell of a brass instrument to soften and change its tone.

OBBLIGATO. An improvised countermelody. In Dixieland style the obbligato is usually performed in a florid, ornamented manner on the clarinet and against the more simple and direct primary theme customarily played by the cornet.

OCTAVE. A unison effect using the same note of a scale in two different registers. Also see *unison*.

OSTINATO. In jazz, usually a repeated bass melody over which chords and a treble melody function.

PARAPHRASE. An ornamented variation or rhythmic variation of an original theme that still bears a recognizable resemblance to the original.

PHRASE. A unit of musical expression, ordinarily four measures in length in pop and jazz tunes, but in an improvised solo it may be any length.

PLAGAL CADENCE. The sound of two consecutive chords, the first a chord built on the fourth degree of a scale in any given key, followed by a chord built on the first degree of the scale. Example: An F chord to a C chord in the key of C.

POLYRHYTHM. A composite of several individual rhythmic patterns performed simultaneously.

QUARTER TONES. Smaller pitch differentials than those found on the piano keyboard between two adjacent notes.

QUOTE. To insert a borrowed fragment of a well-known melody into an improvised solo.

RAGGING. A type of melodic paraphrase. The original contour of the tune is retained but the original rhythm is made more syncopated and irregular.

RAGTIME. One of the earliest definitive jazz styles and primarily a piano style. It was one of the first published types of jazz and was disseminated worldwide for public consumption.

REEDS. Denotes any of the saxophones, clarinets, or flutes.

REGISTER. The low, middle, or high ranges of sounds produced by an instrument.

RHYTHM SECTION. Most often piano, bass, and drums. Guitar is also common. So called because in the big swing band there was a sax section, a trumpet section, and a trombone section. The instruments that mostly comped and kept time were called the rhythm section.

RIFF. A simple repeated melodic idea, usually two or four measures in length and often used in the 12-bar blues format. The ensemble plays the riff behind and in support of the improvised solo.

RUNS. Scales, scale fragments or chord arpeggiations performed in a rapid or running manner.

SCALE. A set of related tones, usually seven or eight in a series, and usually displayed on the musical staff in an ascending or descending line. This group of related tones helps the listener to determine the key note and the major or minor color of a melody. The scale tones may also be used to construct chords that will establish a tonal center or key center. Also see *key*.

SCAT SINGING. To sing a jazz line or melody using nonsense words or syllables or vocal effects.

SEQUENCE. A set of tones played melodically and then repeated in an ascending or descending pattern.

SESSION. An open improvising contest (jam session), a rehearsal, or a recording studio date.

SITTING IN. Participating in a jam session or performance.

STAGE BAND. (BIG BAND) The standard large jazz ensemble. Consists of a group of saxophones, a group of trumpets, a group of trombones, and a group of pulse and chording instruments called the rhythm section. Evolved from the instrumentation of early swing bands.

STEAL. To borrow a fragment from another melody or quote a favorite cliché of another player.

STRIDE. A piano style which probably evolved from Ragtime. Generally performed faster and with more power and swing feel than Ragtime.

SYNCOPATION. The stress or emphasis of what is normally a weak beat or weak portion of a beat occurring within a steady pulse framework.

SYNTHESIZER. An electronic keyboard instrument that can imitate woodwind, brass, or string sounds.

THEME AND VARIATIONS. An initial tune (theme) followed immediately by a series of connected modified versions of the theme called variations. The modifications may be minimal or radical, but each variation will still bear some structural resemblance to the original theme.

TIME. (in time) Steady, regular pulse, played or implied. Time is usually kept by the drummer but all jazz instrumentalists must develop a good sense of time and must solo in time.

TREMOLO. Common for keyboard, guitar, and bass technique, the rapid reiteration of a tone, sometimes in octaves.

UNISON. The same tone or tones performed simultaneously by two or more different instruments.

VIBRATO. An expressive factor added to the basic pitch of a tone so that it wavers or flutters with an even pulsation.

WALKING BASS. A style of bass playing wherein the bassist plays a note squarely on every beat of every measure, in an ascending or descending scale-like pattern.

NOTES

CHAPTER 7

1. Whitney Balliett, "Number Twenty-six," *The New Yorker Magazine* (July 21, 1980), pp. 90, 91.

CHAPTER 9

1. Malcolm E. Bessom, "Overtones," *Music Educators Journal* (January 1980), pp. 5, 6.
2. Zan Stewart, "Griffin," *Musician, Player & Listener* (January 1, 1979), p. 49.
3. Nat Hentoff, *The Jazz Life* (New York: Da Capo Press, 1975), p. 208.
4. Richmond Browne, in Jerry Coker's *Improvising Jazz* (Englewood Cliffs, New Jersey: Prentice-Hall, 1964), pp. 15, 16.
5. Bill Dobbins, "Improvisation: An Essential Element of Musical Proficiency," *Music Educators Journal* (January 1980), pp. 40, 41.
6. Leroi Jones, album notes for *Four for Trane, Archie Shepp,* Impulse A-71.

BIBLIOGRAPHY

CHILTON, JOHN. *Who's Who of Jazz*. Philadelphia: Chilton Book Company, 1970.

COKER, JERRY. *Improvising Jazz*. Englewood Cliffs, N.J.: Prentice-Hall, Inc., 1964.

COKER, JERRY. *The Jazz Idiom*. Englewood Cliffs, N.J.: Prentice-Hall, Inc, 1975.

COKER, JERRY. *Listening to Jazz*. Englewood Cliffs, N.J.: Prentice Hall, Inc., 1978.

DEXTER, DAVE JR. *The Jazz Story*. Englewood Cliffs, N.J.: Prentice Hall, Inc., 1964.

FEATHER, LEONARD. *The New Edition of the Encyclopedia of Jazz*. New York: Horizon Press, 1960.

FEATHER, LEONARD. *The Encyclopedia of Jazz in the Sixties*. New York: Horizon Press, 1967.

FEATHER, LEONARD. *The Encyclopedia of Jazz in the Seventies*. New York: Horizon Press, 1976.

GRIDLEY, MARK C. *Jazz Styles*. Englewood Cliffs, N.J.: Prentice Hall, Inc., 1978.

HENTOFF, NAT. *The Jazz Life*. New York, N.Y.: Da Capo Press, Inc., 1978.

LEVEY, JOSEPH. *Basic Jazz Improvisation*. Delaware Water Gap, Pa.: Shawnee Press, Inc., 1971.

OSTRANSKY, LEROY. *Jazz City*. Englewood Cliffs, N.J.: Prentice Hall, Inc., 1978.

OSTRANSKY, LEROY. *Understanding Jazz*. Englewood Cliffs, N.J.: Prentice Hall, Inc., 1977.

PLEASANTS, HENRY. *Serious Music—And All That Jazz!* New York: Simon and Schuster, 1969.

RIVELLI, PAULINE AND LEVIN, ROBERT, eds. *Black Giants*. New York: The World Publishing Company, 1970.

RUSSELL, ROSS. *Jazz Style in Kansas City and the Southwest*. Berkeley: University of California Press, 1971.

RUST, BRIAN. *The American Dance Band and Discography*. New Rochelle, N.Y.: Arlington House, 1976.

SHAPIRO, NAT AND HENTOFF, NAT, eds. *Hear Me Talkin' to Ya*. New York: Rinehart and Company, Inc., 1955.

SIMON, GEORGE T. *The Big Bands* (revised edition). New York: Macmillan Publishing Company, Inc., 1974.

SOUTHERN, EILEEN. *The Music of Black Americans*. New York: W. W. Norton and Company, Inc., 1971.

STEARNS, MARSHALL. *The Story of Jazz*. New York: Oxford University Press, 1970.

TIRRO, FRANK. *Jazz: A History*. New York: W. W. Norton and Company, Inc., 1977.

WILDER, ALEC. *American Popular Song*. New York: Oxford University Press, 1972.

WILLIAMS, MARTIN. *Jazz Masters in Transition, 1957-69*. New York: Macmillan Company, 1970.

WILSON, JOHN S. *Jazz: The Transition Years*. New York: Appleton-Century-Crofts, 1966.